PRAISE FOR MARIEn

INNOVATION IS NOTHING WITHOUT COURAGE TO UNLEASH IT

I0048864

"Hits the spot for entrepreneurs and ambitious business owners. This is the kind of wisdom that turns ideas into action."

—C. Michaels,
Founder & CEO, Visionary Leadership Group

"Dr. Zanyk outdoes regular entrepreneurial books by offering specific and effective insights rooted in real-world experience. A must-read for innovators and dreamers alike!"

—R. Belmont,
National Branding Executive

"A refreshing take on business innovation—
equal parts wisdom and inspiration."

—Dr. C. Hennings,
Professor of Business Strategy

"An immersive and satisfying read, full of practical guidance and motivational stories that will inspire anyone to take their business to the next level."

—K. Barnes,
Senior Contributor, Entrepreneurial Review

"An authentic, amusing, and inspiring read for anyone who needs a boost of courage when facing life's challenges. Zanyk's journey is both relatable and extraordinary. I look forward to more from her company ZANEEZ®"

—**M. Renner,**
Executive VP, Global Marketing Solutions

"In a sea of business books, Zanyk's voice stands out for its honesty, humor, and hands-on advice."

—**L. Tate,**
Senior Analyst, Financial Insight Advisors

PUBLICATIONS & MEDIA HIGHLIGHTS

1. Featured Successes & Media Highlights

- **737UConn Today**—*Getting a Foot Up on Production Simulation and Streamlining*
  A profile on the cutting-edge virtual prototyping of AnkleSTONE® in collaboration with UConn's Manufacturing Simulation Center.

- **Forge Impact**—*ZANEEZ®: Success Story—Ph.D.'s Biomimetic Devices Heal the World... Ankle First.*
  Showcases the inspiration and development behind AnkleSTONE® nd Dr. Zanyk's journey to commercial viability.

- **Harvest Growth**—*How Courage and Perseverance Helped This Entrepreneur Succeed—AnkleSTONE®* (Sept 2023)

An inspiring feature on Dr. Zanyk's entrepreneurial path, resilience, and traction with pro sports deals.

- **L.E.R. Magazine**—*Foot and Ankle Therapeutic Device* (Mar 2022) Highlights AnkleSTONE®'s design, portability, and therapeutic value across diverse user groups.

- **WebWire / ALA Conference 2025**—*Trailblazing Author and Orthopedic Innovator Dr. Marien J. Zanyk* Announced Dr. Zanyk's keynote appearance, spotlighting her dual role as author and innovator.

2. Press Releases & Launch Announcements

- **PR Newswire**—*ZANEEZ® Health & Fitness Set to Improve Foot & Ankle Mobility, Flexibility & Health with AnkleSTONE®* (Nov 2021) The official product launch, outlining AnkleSTONE®'s goals and functionality in aiding mobility and injury prevention.

- **Yahoo News**—*AnkleSTONE: Coolest Thing Made in Connecticut* A news video spotlight highlighting AnkleSTONE® as a standout local innovation produced with Watertown Plastics.

3. Authored Works

- **Children's Literature**—*Emu on the Loose* (April 2025); MindStir Media.

  - *When Magic Stirs the Forest* (November 2025); Noble Works Media
  - *Wild Water, Brave Hearts* (coming 2026); DrZanyk.com

- **Business Title**—*Innovation Is NOTHING Without Courage to Unleash It!* (April 2025)

4. Academic & Scientific Publications

- **Cytometry** (1988): Flow cytometric analysis of tumor cell line phenotypic changes following TPA induction.

- **Carcinogenesis** (1988): Transferrin receptor and 4F2 expression in NK-sensitive vs NK-resistant tumor cell lines.

- **Analytical Cell Pathology** (1990): Flow cytometric assay for target binding by NKH1A$^+$ cells.

- **Cytopathology** (1990): Immunogold labeling of tumor cells during NK/target interactions.

5. Intellectual Property & Innovation Portfolio

Issued Utility & Design Patents:

- *WillowWORX® Freestyle Station* (2018)

- *AnkleSTONE® Pain & Conditioning Solution* (2019)

- *BedROK® Mobility Mat* (2019)

- *BaseROK®* (2019; refiled 2023)

INNOVATION

is

NOTHING,

without

COURAGE

to

UNLEASH IT

ENTREPRENEURIAL EMPOWERMENT, STRATEGIES AND SECRETS FOR SUCCESS

Dr. Marien J. Zanyk PhD

Copyright © 2025 Dr. Marien J. Zanyk, PhD

Paperback: 978-1-968519-41-4
Hardback: 978-1-968519-42-1
Ebook: 978-1-968519-43-8

All rights reserved. No part of this publication may be reproduced, distributed, or transmitted in any form or by any electronic or mechanical means, without the prior written permission of the publisher, except in the case of brief quotations embodied in critical reviews and certain other noncommercial uses permitted by copyright law.

Ordering Information:

Books to Life Marketing
KNOW YOUR BOOK'S PURPOSE TO LIFE

Books to Life Marketing Ltd
128 City Road, London, EC1V 2NX, UK

Printed in the United States of America

For my dear Dad, Joseph Zanyk—
my source of innovation and inspiration.

For my mom, Kathreen—
who inspired my love of reading and lifelong joy.

CONTENTS

In the world of healthcare, a persistent gap often separates
the tools available from the outcomes desired. Yet within
this challenge we can embrace the opportunity to push
boundaries, and revel in the transformative power
of innovation.

Finding herself in a healthcare situation, as Consultant in
musculoskeletal recovery, that revealed itself to be devoid of
anatomically assistive solutions, and littered with makeshift
remedies, the author considered how to make the situation
better in pushing the boundaries of Orthopedic health to
include Interactive Orthopedic exercise platforms, that we
believe not only heal bodies, but can restore lives.

The author's childhood experience at Niagara Falls becomes
a metaphor for her entrepreneurial path: to fortify yourself
with an unyielding self-belief.

Chapter 7 ushers us into the world of a Connecticut-based startup that aims to redefine orthopedic solutions with platforms that support your body, in the *correct* 'ultimate' position, so you can do the exercise correctly, every time. Here, readers are introduced to a lineup of cutting-edge orthopedic products, designed through Bioscience body mechanics technology, in contoured exercise platforms, to enhance body conditioning, prevent injury, and expedite recovery. The groundbreaking innovations under the ZANEEZ® Health umbrella include: AnkleSTONE®, BedROK®, BaseROK®, and WillowWORX®. Visit us at AnkleSTONE.com and ZANEEZ.com.

Chapter 8 is a roadmap that details the journey of transforming ideas into tangible products. A product development pathway that starts in USA, with production elements in Canada and China, and a return back to the East coast of USA, where the business is taking root, this story exemplifies support, self-empowerment, self-love, and the sheer art of manifestation. Aiming to shed light on essential elements like ingenuity, perseverance, confidence, financial aspects, courage, vision, consistency, longevity, credibility, creativity, happiness, and gratitude, which accumulate to lead to empowerment.

As we explore the vast opportunities of these new devices within the orthopedic market, from professional sports to medical rehabilitation, readers discover how ZANEEZ® aims to fill unmet needs in this industry, providing readers with valuable insight into entrepreneurial strategies.

CHAPTER 10

Building a Team—Attracting Partners with 'Skin in the Game'

> Chapter 10 narrates the evolution toward building a dedicated team that shares our universal goals and ambitions. The significance of attracting individuals who have "skin in the game" and are committed to long-term mutual rewards is explored.

CHAPTER 11

Strategies for Success—9 Key Considerations

> Readers gain access to key lessons learned by Dr. Zanyk on her entrepreneurial journey. These lessons span from how to heighten and hold your courage, to the importance of high resonance, to the benefits of reading facial & body language, and mixed in with impactful work strategies for achieving success.

CHAPTER 12

The Power of Resonance—Harnessing Positive Energy.

> Within a pivotal theme, we explore the concept of resonance and the role it plays in attracting what one needs to understand the energy field and your own abilities to create positive resonance.

CHAPTER 13

Reading the World—Mastering the Communication of Body and Facial Language.

> Referring to the art of interpreting body language in macro- and micro-expressions, Chapter 13 offers readers insights into effective communication strategies, providing a "master class" in advantageous skill sets, especially necessary in the business world. This mastery allows for a deeper understanding of human interactions and improves the accuracy of your interpretation of unspoken thoughts.

Lessons learned focuses on the art of articulation,
emphasizing brevity and tolerance in communication,
shedding light on recognizing gender-based differences in
language usage and the impact it has in various contexts.

Underscoring the importance of adopting the right
perspective to attract your audience, readers are encouraged
to let go of the product and embrace the dream, the dream
of the customers. It reveals why and how you should
respect the range and need for brevity with 'plain speak' in
communication. How to "Boil it Down" to grab your audience.

Small, persistent steps toward one's vision and goals,
reinforce the path to significant victories.

In Chapter 17 readers are introduced to the transformative
power of strategic mentorship. Shared insights into the role
mentors play and how mentorship can be a game-changer
for aspiring entrepreneurs.

Taking action, and its role in bringing ideas to fruition,
enables executive actions for tangible results.

PROLOGUE

In the world of healthcare, a persistent gap often separates the tools available from the outcomes desired. Yet within this challenge resides a remarkable opportunity for innovation and transformation. It is within the depths of this challenge that we find the fertile ground for pushing boundaries and achieving extraordinary results.

As an Orthopedic Consultant, at the forefront of this struggle, witnessing frustrations with a void in post injury rehabilitation. In a journey to create alternative solutions to primitive props disguised as exercise aids, the quest for effective movement restoration was undertaken for individuals seeking relief from injury or post-surgery to athletes striving for peak performance. But amidst this challenge affecting injured patients and athletes and everyone in between just looking for pain free, musculoskeletal function, lies an opportunity for innovation and transformation.

The strategies and powers that enable us to break through these barriers are fueled by a belief that transcends other boundaries. Dr. Zanyk invites you to discover strategies and secrets for successful propulsion towards your goals and aspirations.

CHAPTER 1

The Innovation Imperative

Have you ever found yourself in a healthcare situation, or any impactful situation, that wasn't going very well, where you just knew—deep down—that you could make the situation so much better? You could envision improving the outcome, probably changing lives too.

Well, I sure have.

As an Orthopedic Consultant, working alongside surgeons, therapists, and patients to restore movement in affected joints, I witnessed firsthand the frustration and despair caused by very limited tools, typically props, ineffective as exercise aids.

Primitive at best—inferior and makeshift remedies for feet and ankles like tennis balls, rubber bands, slanted blocks, and for the whole body and frozen joints, stretch cages, and a lot of wishful thinking. We were all constantly searching for a fulcrum to impact the movement. It was lacking.

From what I've seen, this void seems to affect everyone. And it's not just about discomfort—it's a significant healthcare challenge in which billions of dollars are spent each year on ineffective solutions that don't address the root cause.

From injured, rock-hard knees—to locked up ankles, frozen shoulders, and backs begging for relief—to athletes with inevitable injury or just regular people who are feeling sore and overworked by life and need to condition themselves to rejuvenate.

Consider the patient who survived a motorcycle wreck, left with a body in desperate need of repair—full of screws, rivets, & plates holding him together. The challenge? To get him moving again and with *no* pain. Frustration mounted with outdated methods, such as using the stairs for his rock-hard contracted ankle, the arm of the couch to mobilize his stiff contracted knees, perhaps with a high tech 'bag of rice' to weigh the limb down. Too often the door frame, which holds up a house, was offered as the primary method to assist a frozen shoulder. Referrals were given for strap-on night splints, most often 'flung off' in the night, or $600 a month rented stretching devices, if you could afford it. It was a problem.

Knowing that total knee replacements & shoulder surgeries are to increase 600% by the year 2030, soft tissue contracture is a formidable problem. Recognizing that 1.7 billion people worldwide suffer muscular skeletal issues, most often without effective therapeutic remedy, indicates a painful problem.

Then there's the athletic population, those who are constantly sidelined by a diversity of injuries; most often, involving their feet and ankles. After all, you've got to marvel at the explosive foot power of our athletes. From the near ankle-breaking prowess of NBA jump shots to the lightning-fast pivots of MMA fighters, baseball pitchers, tennis, soccer, and hockey players. Consider the sheer power of the launch from Olympic starting blocks. It's all fun and games until you learn of the $1.5 Billion loss every year due to player injury in the top 3 Major league sports—NBA, MLB, NFL—from sprained ankles, Achilles tendinopathy, turf toe, lace bite, muscle imbalances, weak lift-off, and the ubiquitous plantar fasciitis, affecting 8 out of every 10 adults.

Speaking of adults… the 'regular' people, who inevitably suffer life's injuries and ailments or body fatigue; it is apparent that everyone is looking for a decent way to stretch, to relieve pain, and to maintain their functional movement. Millions of people search for convenient methods to keep their bodies supple and need help.

I became motivated to develop a new form of therapy to provide help. Armed with strengths of Orthopedic Science, Biomedical and clinical training, plus the sudden challenge to repair my own knee injury from skiing too hard in Vermont, I developed therapy support tools to fix the problem.

The true twist of fate certainly was the burden of my own knee injury that forced me to find a solution. For my own rehab, I naturally turned to the place I call my "Exercise Haven," a very private running trail, and a natural landscape perfect for body conditioning, hidden in the depths of the Connecticut forest, in a 10,000-acre forest sanctuary in my own backyard. I'm a regular warrior out there in this private forest as I use the fallen tree branches as weights; I use the trees, rocks, and cliffs to gain the angles for aggressive strength & flexibility training. I even use the moss to cushion my wrists during push-ups on the rocks. Basically, I use what nature gave me. Do you know… that I fixed my injured knee using my own form of therapy, within just three weeks; advancing from crutches to a soft run without going to therapy. I discovered that the forest tree, the Mountain Laurel has tree branches that are perfectly spaced as handholds and pliable for resistant strength training, for progressive incremental tissue stretching. I expanded this method, succeeded in my own remarkable recovery, and proved to myself that this method can be duplicated.

The contoured branches inspired the contoured limbs of WillowWORX®, and biomimicry of their material properties and shape, engineered the instant change in resistance. From that spark of inspiration, and proof of efficacy, I realized this can be done. Over the next two years, I set upon: designing, patenting, developing, and field-testing our first innovation, WillowWORX®—a standing exercise station, offering progressive incremental tissue stretching and resistance training and that can replace an entire gym of heavy metal equipment. From there, the entrepreneurial journey gained momentum, with science-based tools. I developed the other products AnkleSTONE®, BedROK®, AND BaseROK®. Bio-Science Body Mechanics (BSBM) benefits have gained traction with NBA, UConn basketball, US soccer, and countless individuals in discovery of the products in prototype and product form.

We've uncovered vast potential within a $7B addressable market hungry for innovation. Not only focusing on athleticism but also on relieving the burden of injury. AnkleSTONE® is contoured to provide optimal leverage for feet and ankles, with its ramps and therapeutic grooves to enable all-in-one precision results. Visit AnkleSTONE.com

BedROK® is unique and purposeful in its design for whole body exercise. It's therapeutic grooves, ramps, and easy-grip ledges provide a lean grip for movement with multi-purpose benefits. You don't need big heavy metal grips and bulky handles, or time-consuming trips to the gym; Instead, like rock climbers, you can use a lean grip with just fingertips, engaging flexor digitorum to stabilize effectively. The round handholds are shaped to accommodate full range of movement to avoid the locked position across the joints. (As is typical when the wrist is extended on the floor for push-ups.) BaseROK® is in development as an exciting assistive platformed mat, with benefits that far exceed a plain exercise mat.

I will continue to push the boundaries of Orthopedic health. As ZANEEZ® Orthopedic platforms symbolize more than a product; they signify a leap towards a healthier, more active future for millions, as we're not just healing bodies; we're restoring lives.

Now is a good time to ask... How do we get here?
At the intersection of innovation and performance, you might wonder, "How does one get here?"

At a stage to translate a real medical need and an idea inspired by nature into commercial viability. First, with an unwavering belief in yourself, and in your vision. Innovation is fueled by a controllable power within, fortified by resonance of unyielding encouragement, love, gratitude, and pure belief in yourself!

How else will you light the path? As you climb over challenges and step one at a time, toward your vision? The impact of the correct and advanced belief positioning is huge.

In disclosing entrepreneurial empowerment strategies, and secrets for success, and the tips to help you, it is right to focus on the amplification of belief in yourself so strong that it transcends boundaries.

When I was just a little kid of three-and-a half visiting Niagara Falls with my family—perched 200 feet up, I had a transformative experience that proved my ability to be constant on either side of a risk. For me, my discovery at a very young age, revealed that personal capability is the same on either side of the risk. I determined then that I was never going to let myself down.

To propel ourselves forward toward our goals, we require a never give up attitude, and an ability to always find the funny parts in life's absurdities. Innovation is challenging, often a blend of triumph and comedy. Embrace the funny parts and relish them. After all, its not reality that shapes us but the lens through which we view the world that shapes our reality.

As innovators, we must embrace self-belief to succeed, to advance from idea to reality, prototype to product, from innovation to impact.

CHAPTER 2

A Different Perspective—Niagara Falls and the Belief in Oneself That Transcends Boundaries

As mentioned, at the young age of three-and-a-half, while on family holiday, I did find myself perched precariously 200 feet above the thundering chasm of Niagara Falls. I, with the audacity only a child could muster, decided it was time for a change in scenery. The colossal gorge before me was awe-inspiring, but my curiosity beckoned me to explore the other side, to bask in an even grander vista. I was a confident little bugger, a strong and capable little kid who knew that not much could hold her back. I was already an expert at climbing. I had mastered the art, going beyond the confines of cupboard drawers used for covert cookie missions, ascending to the dizzying heights of apple trees in the orchard, and even scaling the neighborhood fences with the confidence that I could conquer any climb without a single scrape or bruise. Perhaps as is typical of the youngest child hierarchy, I had a special confidence that I could climb anything, real and metaphorical.

With my family temporarily distracted—a bustling clan comprised of my mom, my dad, and my trio of older sisters, aged five, nine—and ten, I seized the moment. With a calculated boldness, casting caution aside, I traversed the four-inch diameter brass guard rail. One leg over, then the other, each move executed with the precision of a seasoned acrobatic "tough kid," all the while maintaining a vice-like grip on that fat, cold, metal rail that separated me from my ambitious destination. As I dangled between worlds, my grip never faltered, and I marveled at the sweeping panorama before me. It was a refreshing new view as it had an element of excitement to it. A mere 30 seconds passed before my clandestine endeavor was interrupted by a heart-piercing shriek—my mother had discovered my audacious exploit. In a flash, I found myself grabbed and returned to the "safe" side of the railing, my newfound perspective denied, but not forgotten. My impromptu adventure was met with a barrage of bewildered questions.

"Why? Why in the world would you do such a thing?" And though I couldn't articulate it at the time, that question resonated with me. It echoed throughout my life, and later, I would offer a simple and wholehearted response:

Why wouldn't I?
My ability did not falter from one side of the railing to the other.

Within the context of calculated risks, why not choose to utilize your capabilities to their fullest extent? Why not strive for the extraordinary? Even at that young age, I had instantly measured the risks, calculated the odds, and determined that my ambition outweighed the potential perils. I knew I could and wanted to.

Crossing that metaphorical boundary was a leap toward my aspiration, not a retreat.

The belief in oneself—a conviction so unwavering that it propels you from the inception of an idea to its tangible reality—is a force of nature. It's the impetus that emboldened me to hurdle the precipice of risk, even in adulthood, to grasp the rewards of my ambition. And in those moments suspended between the railing and the abyss, I understood that my capacity to *hold on* remained constant, whether on one side of the guard rail or the other.

Thinking of it logically, the same hands that conquered tree limbs and scaled cupboard shelves had not weakened; they were fortified by my unyielding self-belief. Failure was not an option, not when I had the power to lift myself up. Physically, the muscles in my hands and arms and feet and legs worked the same on either side of the railing. This intrinsic faith, recognition of some basic laws of physics and actual risk, mixed with this audacious self-trust, would continue to thread its way through the tapestry of my life, culminating in ventures that would challenge and, I think, redefine what's possible.

What is it, this unshakeable belief in oneself?

This audacity that propels us from mere contemplation to remarkable realization. It's the foundation upon which we construct our dreams, a belief so profound that it urges us to surmount the risk, to seize the rewards that await on the other side. From the vantage point of that fateful day at Niagara Falls, the concept became crystalline: belief fuels ambition, and ambition propels us beyond the boundaries of fear into the boundless realm of possibility.

CHAPTER 3

Discovering the Power Within—
Harnessing Nature for Healing

You must be brave enough to step into this mindset, in whatever direction your own strengths take you to accomplish your ambitions. The road less traveled leads to stories that shimmer with the rare glow of unconventional accomplishment. My own journey isn't confined to the well-trodden paths of the commonplace; it's an expedition that takes me through my own manifestations and thoughts to do the next step. I am often asking, "ok what's next?" And this lifestyle, the entrepreneurial one, full of push and pull, courage and risk, can be lovely and worth pursuing.

As you strive toward your own goals, it's not just about arriving at a destination, but about savoring each stride of the expedition. I encourage you to celebrate the fusion of your determination, your innovation, and your courage, all of which is sure to culminate in a mosaic that stands as a testament to the road less traveled and the satisfaction found therein.

For over eight years, I have pursued an entrepreneurial odyssey, and found myself navigating a terrain enriched with the currency of self-belief. But I had to make the transactions to deposit consistent belief into my own head. Despite any setbacks or life burdens, my positive thoughts prevail.

My narrative is fueled by Ukrainian tenacity and driven by a boundless hunger for solutions, with a commitment to humor that has helped turn my ambitions into stepping stones toward my goals of commercial production of new orthopedic products. It becomes apparent that your own daring makes a great funny story.

I relied on my Ukrainian spirit to navigate the intricacies of my journey. The threads of unwavering confidence are woven seamlessly alongside the sparks of ambition that are inherently ignited. Through my lens over the years, from initial idea to current business status, I glimpsed a sense of the power of my self-belief and daring ambition, which helped to sculpt not just an inventor but a storyteller and a visionary who has learned to dance in the extraordinary.

Observing the Ukrainian people protect themselves from Russian invasion throughout history, with the intensity of war rising in 2022, has shone a light on my own Ukrainian spirit, striving forward with unrelenting perseverance and humor. Known as an incredible force of independence, and perseverance, the spirit of Ukrainians revealed on the National stage helped others to recognize this unique spirit. Since the war began, when I mention my nationality people respond with a nod and a smile in understanding.

My Grandma, Anastasia, and my dad, Joseph, instilled in me an inner drive that claims a legacy steeped in Ukrainian spirit. A relentless drive urges me to unearth solutions, unravel answers, and find innovations.

My early childhood memories that shape who I am include episodes of being in the basement in my dad's workshop. My ambitions were shaped at age three or four, in an environment that included drills that whirl into chunks of wood and saws that rip a board apart, rows of jars of nails, hammers, and bottles of white glue. Weekends gave me a chance to shadow my dad for a couple of hours as he fixed and built, wired, and cut, drilled, and created *solutions* for our home. Weekday mornings gave me a chance to "play workshop" by myself. With my three older sisters off at school and my dad away at his engineering job, I would grab the opportunity to test out my skills. I wasn't yet old enough to go to school, yet to my mom's credit, despite her surprise whenever she heard me using the power tools, all by myself; she gave me her permission to proceed, if I promised to be careful, despite my being just a little kid. My mom's acknowledgment of my competence permitted me to acquire confidence and so the cycle strengthens. To this day, I say, to people, especially women, you must work with power tools; I say, "go saw some wood", "use a chainsaw," even, "create a project", and "don't be afraid" to use the tools of *power*. The experience of using power tools strengthens you and gives you the confidence to cope with the challenges in home or car maintenance, problem solving, and other challenges within your life's ambitions. Go for the big stuff. Why hold back? Mastering power tools not only empowers women and men with essential skills but also instills a profound sense of bravery, showing that they can confidently handle anything that comes their way. If you can handle and control power tools, you can handle anything and be a "gutsy broad" or warrior at any age.

A special colleague of mine, Barry Ressler, Director of the Space Medicine Consortium, and renowned particle physicist, noticed my "gutsiness" as I presented my first invention and business platform at a New York City Venture Summit, and remarked to me one day, "Marien, I believe you can dance on ceilings!" This has been one of the best compliments of my life. Those words kept me going. Gutsy or competent, focused or driven, dancer on floors or ceilings, either one of those terms is good to hear and a fine way to live. Always...be dancing on the ceiling.

I rely on the power of "positive" to prevent my falling from the ceiling onto the hard floor. As my Ukrainian Grandma Anastasia would have said, "That's the way!" as she consistently remained positive, despite the challenges of the previous century. Born in 1899, Anastasia was no stranger to life's challenges. Whether she was navigating the hardships of farm life, sharing her wisdom on birthing, and raising her 12 children, or simply guiding the perfect amount of butter into her pierogies, "that's the way" embodied her approach to life, as she incorporated her own forcefield to carry on.

You must recognize that within your *own* veins, the blood of your ancestry flows with vigor, and power infusing you with a profound determination. The pursuit of solutions isn't just a choice; it's a calling that resonates deep within, as a call to action. When you listen and respond to it, this ancestral driving force will propel you to tackle your challenges head-on, never swaying in the face of adversity. Well, almost never—you _do_ have permission to sway or falter sometimes, when necessary. But in general, you don't have to be striving to craft groundbreaking innovations that defy the limits of convention, you can just *be* within your own glory, as defined by your own ambitions. Your natural happiness 'set point' can be adjusted to high, and maintained by you, and only you, with determination.

Stirring into the mix of your own driving force, you must add that little thing called humor—what an indomitable ally it proves to be. It's the beacon that guides us back when faced with the formidable. Not to always be laughing, but, yes, always, be laughing.

Recognizing that even the most challenging experiences can be infused with humor is a valuable skill. I often find that sharing these stories with my daughter, three sons, or my sister brings out the hidden laughter. The humor is always there, reminding us that even the most complex problems can be unraveled with a hearty chuckle and a creative perspective. I often add a simple one-liner to my own escapades, or funny dialogue, spoken out loud or just in my head.

By capturing the humor that underlies the absurdity of life, as events most often unravel in the most unpredictable ways, we can turn the crappy parts into comedy and light moments of laughter. The funny bits are always there.

CHAPTER 4

Driven Toward Success— 'Never Give Up' Attitude

perseverance

noun

persistence in doing something despite difficulty or delay in achieving success.
The skill in never giving up.

To inspire you to persevere, to stoke the drive inside you and commit to *never giving up*, imagine this: Excelsior, Minnesota, a sunny day, Triathlon Day, and I'm geared up, after weeks of preparation, to take on a triathlon that involved swimming roughly a mile across a lake, cycling 15 miles of countryside, and running a final five miles to the finish line. I was feeling strong from running and swimming practice and I had borrowed a good-looking bike from a friend. The excitement in the air was palpable, but little did I know the humorous twist fate had in store for me.

After conquering the swim across the lake, being sure to stay at the edge of the pack to avoid the bubbling crowd of hundreds of swimmers who literally swim over each other to get ahead, I emerged in good position on the other side of the lake and headed onto my bike, pedaling away toward the country road racecourse. All was well until, out of nowhere, BOOM! My back tire decided to celebrate the Fourth of July prematurely. The exploding tire tossed me from my bike, and I was thrown hard onto the side of the gravel road. I was immediately stopped in my tracks ... or was I? Some people might have thrown in the towel, but not me. With adrenaline pumping and a mission to accomplish, I surveyed my peculiar surroundings—smack dab in the middle of cornfields. It felt like a scene right out of a rural comedy. Fueled by tenacity, and some might say sheer lunacy, I sprang into action. Picture this: a determined figure adorned with numbers on their chest and back, clad in not-so-flattering bike shorts and skimpy, spandex top, still wet from the lake swim, sprinting across the road, through the cornfield, and over hedges! If there was ever a sitcom moment, this was it, with the Benny Hill theme playing in the background. Finally, panting but unwavering, I reached an old farmhouse. I knocked on that metal door like my race depended on it, and in a way, it did. A man answered, probably wondering why a helmeted maniac was standing at his doorstep. I quickly explained my dire situation, which, to my surprise, he comprehended swiftly, given my attire and the numbers plastered all over me. Now, here's the kicker. This kind soul offered me a bike, but not just any bike. Oh no, it was a bright little number belonging to his 12-year-old son. Complete with tassels, a rear book holder, and perhaps a sprinkle of magic dust, this bike became my lifeline back to the race.

Off I went, wobbling on this pint-sized contraption, careening down the dirt road like a daredevil on training wheels. With just three gears at my disposal, I felt like I'd been transported back to grade school. But I was back in the game, back in the race, back with a vengeance—or should I say, with a hearty chuckle.

As I sped along, I couldn't contain my laughter. It bubbled up from deep within, and I had to stifle it to avoid tumbling off my juvenile vehicle. The image of a grown-up person on a pint-sized bike with a book holder and tassels, zipping along like the world's most determined Olympian, still makes me laugh. Determination is a powerful energy.

Finally, I crossed the finish line to the looks of confusion from my waiting family—they'd been patient due to my tire mishap. Crossing that line on that quirky bike was a moment of triumph and comedy intertwined. Bewilderment danced in the eyes of those who witnessed my bicycle, and then admiration as they figured out what had happened. Laughing along with their surprise, I ditched my bike, and sped into the running leg of the race to finish with respect. To this day, I am proud that I'd completed the triathlon, and I did it with style, tassels, and all.

I recounted this tale of hilarity for years to come. So, there you have it, a heart full of laughter and the face of triumph. The comedy of life transferred with us from Minnesota to Connecticut, as I relocated my entire family of multiple kids and many pets to the East Coast.

In the forested regions of New England, my backyard is 10,000 acres of forest. The vast expanse of nature, spanning thousands of acres, is unique. For me, the forest is a place of tranquil beauty and the inspiration for an entire lineup of professional orthopedic devices being brought to market.

It is exciting to share the immense market potential for ZANEEZ products, starting with professional sports and expanding to medical rehabilitation, injury prevention, and recovery. The target audience includes orthopedic specialists, pain management clinicians, athletes, trainers, patients, podiatrists, rehabilitation centers, gyms, military, and distributors, among others. The prevalence of musculoskeletal issues necessitates effective solutions, and ZANEEZ is dedicated to making a lasting impact on the lives of millions affected by these conditions, ultimately improving their quality of life.

Our solution revolves around exercise platforms that are meticulously designed to cater to the anatomical condition. These platforms aren't just tailored to your anatomy; they're also constructed using Bio-Science Body Mechanics (BSBM) technology. Inspired by nature, our products are backed by patents and registered trademarks, grounded in scientific principles, and rigorously field-tested. Currently, we've successfully completed the initial manufacturing phase in Connecticut, and we're poised to venture into an underserved $7 billion marketplace, that is hungry for innovation.

I will claim that it took strength, grit *and humor* to get us here.

CHAPTER 5

From Idea to Reality—An Entrepreneurial Journey Fueled by Self-Belief and a Passion for Orthopedic Innovation

At ZANEEZ® Health, we are driven by a mission to revolutionize the way we approach orthopedic health, as our vision is to elevate musculoskeletal fitness for peak performance and recovery. We craft cutting-edge orthopedic devices that harness precise anatomical alignment for calculated outcomes—a realm previously unexplored.

It is a pleasure to share these stories with you, as CEO and founder of ZANEEZ®, to introduce you to our line of four orthopedic products, and to share some stories to illuminate independence, tenacity, and strength, mixed with endurance, some courage, and a clear vision.

At ZANEEZ, we believe in empowering you to "Move the Way You're Meant To." Our unwavering commitment is directed toward addressing the unmet needs of body conditioning and injury recovery, with an aim to enhance the lives of countless individuals worldwide.

We have meticulously crafted four Orthopedic Exercise Innovations: AnkleSTONE®, BedROK®, BaseROK®, and WillowWORX®, with the potential to revolutionize the $7 billion fitness device industry. Visit our new sites AnkleSTONE.COM and ZANEEZ.COM.

Crafted to perfectly complement your anatomy, the ZANEEZ "tools" provide correct support for ultimate correct exercise positions, for multiple needs within a fitness journey. These exercise platforms offer targeted precision, unparalleled comfort, and the ability to unlock the full range of motion in all your joints.

ZANEEZ products feature innovative grips for enhanced leverage, supportive ramps, therapeutic grooves, ledges and versatile roll bars,— all catering to your flexibility and resistance strength training needs. The tools introduce fresh angles, elevate the challenges posed to your joints, and promise more than just fitness—they offer an opportunity for transformative improvement.

In an era in which maintaining peak fitness, flexibility, and pain-free, unrestricted movement is of paramount importance, our vision to establish the world's preeminent company dedicated to creating elegantly simple, yet profoundly comprehensive tools, will empower people to stretch and fortify their bodies.

Flexibility, targeted conditioning, and pain-free, unrestricted movement is of paramount importance, and we are driven by an unrelenting passion to not only meet but exceed the expectations of our valued customers. We strive to provide them with the finest "tools" that will elevate their body conditioning to new heights, encompassing every joint and soft tissue.

CHAPTER 6

The Problem and the Solution— Unveiling the Prevalence of Musculoskeletal Issues; The Void in Effective Conditioning and Recovery Tools

Musculoskeletal problems afflict a staggering 1.7 billion people across 160 countries worldwide. These issues encompass a broad spectrum of conditions including joint pain and stiffness, back pain, arthritis, and various injuries that affect the bones, muscles, ligaments, tendons, and other supporting structures of the body. While it's a given that humans will inevitably experience injuries and may require surgical interventions throughout their lives, the real issue stems from the lack of effective tools for both conditioning and post-injury recovery that genuinely cater to the intricacies of human anatomy. The problem lies in the absence of effective conditioning and injury recovery tools that truly address these anatomical complexities.

As a scientist and orthopedic specialist, I find it disheartening to witness the pervasive problem of musculoskeletal issues affecting almost 2 billion people worldwide. Methods recommended by doctors and trainers are often subpar, leading to suffering. The world is in dire need of proper solutions.

AnkleSTONE is the only All-in-One foot and ankle conditioning platform that has the potential to revolutionize how athletes train, patients recover, and individuals maintain optimal musculoskeletal health. By leveraging cutting-edge technology and thoughtful design, ZANEEZ offers a comprehensive solution to address the challenges faced by both professionals and everyday people. With a robust marketing strategy and a commitment to collaboration with medical professionals, therapists, trainers, and distributors, ZANEEZ is set to make a significant impact on the $7 billion fitness/wellness device market. We aim to counter the prevailing issue of widespread and noticeable lack of effective conditioning and injury recovery tools for corrective exercise and rehabilitation. Improvised methods of using an old tennis ball, collapsible water bottle or the basic wall are ineffective and the entire world is in dire need of proper solutions.

These issues not only cause immense physical discomfort but also significantly impact individuals' quality of life, hindering their ability to perform daily activities and affecting their mental well-being. From the elderly seeking relief from arthritic pain to young athletes battling sports injuries, the burden of musculoskeletal issues touches lives across all age groups and demographics.

The statistics speak for themselves: In the United States alone, 65 million Americans grapple with back pain issues, and eight out of ten adults suffer from foot and ankle problems. Ankle injuries are alarmingly common. Daily, 35,000 ankle sprains occur, making foot and ankle injuries one of the most common in sports. The demand for innovative and effective conditioning tools is higher than ever, as people search for new and better solutions, and we are uniquely positioned to fill this void with our groundbreaking products for better sports medical results.

As an orthopedic specialist, I have found that as the prevalence of musculoskeletal problems continues to rise, promoting preventive measures and public awareness becomes more crucial. My mission is to alleviate the suffering caused by these conditions and improve patients' overall musculoskeletal health through smart orthopedic devices for independent, personalized treatment, vital in helping patients regain mobility, function, and independence. Moreover, educating individuals about proper body mechanics, exercise, and ergonomics can help reduce the risk of musculoskeletal injuries and improve overall musculoskeletal health.

Collaboration between medical professionals, researchers, and policymakers is vital in addressing the global impact of musculoskeletal issues. By sharing knowledge and resources, we can develop innovative solutions and implement effective strategies to combat these prevalent conditions. Together, through dedication and collective effort, we can bring relief and healing to the millions affected by musculoskeletal problems, ultimately improving the quality of life for countless individuals around the globe.

My Story—Filling the Void in Conditioning & Recovery

From natural scientist to business strategist and inventor, I began my career as an orthopedic specialist collaborating closely with both physicians and their patients. I had a front-row seat to the challenges that people face with musculoskeletal issues and trauma. The frustration stemming from acute and chronic stiffness, pain, and a lack of suitable tools for self-conditioning was palpable. Our attempts to engineer effective fulcrums to position and exercise the joint often fell short of the mark, leaving a contracted joint where movement used to occur. It was a problem that also presented as an opportunity for innovation.

Then I became aware that the world of athletes faced its own set of dilemmas. As financial stakes are high—millions of dollars are dependent upon optimal musculoskeletal performance—it was astonishing to discover that $1.4 billion is lost annually, in the top three major league sports, basketball, baseball and football, due to athlete injuries. This predicament is exacerbated by the reality that solutions to truly address anatomical intricacies have not yet been available, frequently forcing clinicians and trainers to recommend subpar or makeshift remedies. The old fallbacks, recommendations to use a ball or 'collapsible' water bottle for foot and ankle recovery is primitive, outdated, ineffective, and truly under-serving to the patient and athlete.

In a twist of fate, my own knee injury from skiing became the catalyst for a groundbreaking revelation that led me to create a standing exercise station, based on the shapes and functions of the trees I used in the forest on my runs.

While downhill skiing in Vermont, obviously too aggressively, I injured my knee, rendering severe pain and massive swelling, and my mobility constrained to the aid of crutches. Following an examination by an orthopedic surgeon, I was determined to heal myself. After all, I was an orthopedic physical therapist, and held extensive knowledge of anatomy from human dissection, and a few autopsies, acquired during my studies in Pathology.

I live in a remarkable piece of Connecticut, and I have what feels like a forest belonging just to me and the animals that dwell here. A natural path extends as far as I want to go, potentially leading as far as 30 miles straight south to the ocean. For years, I have jogged past the dense trees, cliffs, and thick ferns, on a perfect four-foot-wide path. The trail is surrounded by a canopy of towering trees, adorned with oaks, evergreens, and Mountain laurel, and the serenading sounds of silence, or birdsong, as I immerse myself in the incredible beauty that's both enchanting and tranquil.

I have puzzled over the origin of this path for years. How does such a well-groomed trail exist, deep within the forest, as if magically placed there?

This trail is not just a path but a testament to the enduring power of nature. It's likely an ancient riverbed, its topography guiding rainwater down the Connecticut hills for millennia. Over 10,000 years, or even 100,000 years or more, fresh forest soil has filled in, and now, I run on the top of the remnants of this riverbed. The natural flow of rainwater down the Connecticut hills continues to groom the trails, clearing the leaves and debris for me and shaping the landscape as it has for ages.

These well-groomed, *soft* forest floor running trails not only cushion my joints during my long runs but are a testament to nature's offerings of unique and captivating experiences. All of the elements of the forest serve as parts of my versatile, organic gym, including the tree limbs and the moss-covered rocks for "cushioned" leverage.

Natural invention based on need: Within this natural sanctuary, my own, private, versatile, and organic gym, the forest provides an ideal setting for a wide range of exercises: tree limbs and branches become a bar to offer resistance for strength training and provide a means for balanced stretches with progressive grip levels. I even use the fallen tree branches as weights across my shoulders. I often climb into toppled trees that had reached over 40 feet tall and as big as 4 feet in diameter at their trunk, to explore controlled, therapeutic stretches using their branches like an unlimited stretching device. These exercises are performed from hanging positions at various angles, at the *end* of range, targeting the attachment points of soft tissue to the bone, where the stretch is needed most.

The specific properties of the branches of the Mountain laurel, the Connecticut state tree, include a certain push-back characteristic that makes them exceptionally good for resistance strength training. I cured my knee injury with progression therapy using their multi-positioned limbs, which provided positions, support, and resistance strength exercise to promote tissue and range of motion recovery for my legs and whole body.

In addition to the natural benefits of the trees, rocks offer exceptional exercise devices, as they transform into platforms for controlled therapeutic exercises, each with its own outcrops for grips and ledges for advanced positions.

Moss serves as an ideal cushion for push-ups on the rugged, yet ideally shaped, rocks. Using these natural tools, I advanced my therapeutic stretch and strengthening program.

Remarkably, within just three weeks of this natural exercise program I propelled from a state of injury to 95% recovered, as testified by my ability to enjoy a "soft" run in the forest, **_without_** the need for formal therapy.

I recognized that this short-term recovery was quite remarkable and that's when it hit me, that *this can be done,* and I set out to duplicate the therapeutic recovery that the forest provides naturally. I envisioned and designed the first WillowWORX® upright exercise station, described as a mahogany colored, 'tree-like' structure, with therapeutic limbs, grips, handholds, and 'resistance' strength training properties in its 'limbs' mimicking Mountain laurel limb tension. I pursued the patents to secure my claim for this inaugural project. Once the first provisional patents were securely obtained and trademarks registered, these science-based, field-tested creations became positioned to make a significant impact to revolutionize the way we move, within an underserved market for injury recovery and prevention.

Biomimicry was the guiding principle for ZANEEZ products, inspiring not just functional tools, but instruments of grace and efficiency, much like the natural world itself. Nature is the supreme architect and engineer, showcasing a blend of form and function that has captivated human imagination for centuries. Biomimicry, taking cues from nature's ingenious designs, offers a profound lens through which we can re-envision advanced human-made creations.

Biomimetics, as described by science is 'inspiration elicited from nature to design practical materials and systems that can imitate the structure and function of native biological systems. (Sarikaya et al., 2003). More simply put, dragonflies inspiring helicopters and seed pods to Velcro, natural forest to lean interactive design, all lending themselves well to human function and functional wellness. The engineered design with seamless integration of nature's design prowess, offers users tools that are both effective and ergonomic, natural, and desirable to use. Often the answer lies within nature's designs, so let this encourage us to explore the rich offerings of nature, not only for our physical well-being but also for our spiritual growth.

CHAPTER 7

ZANEEZ®—Move the Way You're Meant To—Orthopedic Products Designed to Improve Body Conditioning, with Targeted Positions

As an orthopedic specialist working with patients suffering musculoskeletal conditions post injury and surgery, I grappled with the challenges of various musculoskeletal issues and trauma. I understood the need to create a 'tool' that could serve to facilitate movement, but such a solution was elusive.

Athletes confront a substantial risk when it comes to musculoskeletal performance. Optimal functioning of the musculoskeletal system is paramount, given that millions of dollars are on the line. The well-being of the feet is a critical factor in virtually every sport imaginable.

Clinicians and trainers are frequently left with limited options failing to effectively target the complexities of human anatomy and the generic makeshift remedies underserve the population. Balls roll away and are made for the tennis or lacrosse game; water bottles may cool the foot, but are ineffective, and undesirable especially when they explode on your carpet. In cases of knee contractures, or shoulder stiffness, or various joint mobility issues, people often resort to basic makeshift remedies, such as using walls, towels, Thera bands™, or overnight stretching contraptions, none of which align with the anatomical condition.

Being an inventive soul, receptive to new experiences and relentless in my pursuit of adventure and fitness, I discerned unlimited potential in the ode to creativity, combining physical therapy, anatomy, and the natural world. To make the transition from the vantage point of an orthopedic specialist to that of an entrepreneur reshaping the fitness landscape underscores the boundless potential that comes with aligning ourselves with nature's wisdom.

What sets the ZANEEZ approach apart is the ability to adapt and elevate exercises using elements from nature through biomimicry to suit the anatomical need.

CHAPTER 8

Building from IDEA to Prototype to Product—The Journey of Bringing Ideas to Life

In the heart of Connecticut, I was becoming a visionary inventor embarking on a journey to transform a mere idea into reality. This challenge began with the need to duplicate the physical "push back" property of Mountain laurel, which is different from oak, pine, maple, or any tree, really. If you bend the branches of a Mountain laurel, you feel their unique tension in their trunk and branches, as they match the force you apply and push back with an intensity equal to your force. So, to strengthen your arms, you simply push onto the limbs, in sets of 10 to 20 repetitions, to create resistance strength exercises that are gentler for your joints than heavy weights by far, and effective in matching the amount of intensity your body needs to challenge and strengthen your limbs. It can be a very aggressive work out if you choose the point of high resistance. To change or reduce the amount of intensity, you can simply slide your hand along the length of the limb toward the narrow tip.

Bentwood lamination, a beautiful art and science, was the key in duplicating the properties of this special tree. To create the envisioned WillowWORX Standing Platform, which had been designed and engineered, assigned provisional patent protection, and was ready to be made, my search began with the exploration of bentwood lamination experts, a technique that held the potential to replicate the resistance and flexibility of the branches of Mountain laurel.

A prototype of a single limb was meticulously crafted by the skilled hands of woodcrafter #1 in Connecticut. To my surprised joy, this "bentwood laminator" was able to produce exactly what I had in mind, in the form of one limb. Think of a flexible bow, as in bow and arrow, but with a unique sculpted shape. Proving this could be accomplished with multiple layers of bent maple wood, specifically 7 layers of 2mm thick wood, sandwiched together, and shaped to form a contoured artificial tree branch, I was very confident to advance to the next step.

Crafted from light maple, the limb felt soft, smooth and silky to the touch; elegant, as I slid my hands along its length, rising up the gentle curve and falling down the crest, feeling the changes in resistance toward the narrow-rounded tip. This limb was the perfect prototype to advance the project.

Subsequently, the entire structure was entrusted to the expertise of boat builder #2 in Vermont, renowned for his mastery of Bentwood lamination in large boat construction, producing artisan sailing vessels, and specializing in complex wooden steering wheels.

I traveled up to Vermont several times over six months to his workshop driving through a bumpy, muddy heavily wooded road to monitor the progress. We collaborated successfully on the project and were able to create the first WillowWORX device with properties to match exactly what I had imagined.

I brought home the invention and proudly began to introduce it to potential users. Proof of concept was accomplished quickly, with positive response from all who tested the apparatus as I attended Innovation Summits, conferences, and start up showcases throughout the East coast. I recognized that to realize my vision on a grand scale, with cost efficiency, I would have to seek another production method. Leveraging the invaluable network that I had built within the startup ecosystem within Boston, I secured an introduction to the ultimate bentwood lamination champions, boat builders in Nova Scotia, Canada. It took a few emails and phone calls, as I conveyed the essence of my vision to create the next iteration of the WillowWORX upright exercise device, and to my relief, they acknowledged that it could be done and agreed to work on the project. The quest led me to the ultimate wood craftsman #3, Covey Island Boat Works, renowned as world's finest boat builders, nestled in picturesque Lunenburg, Nova Scotia,

A journey with my daughter, Julia, took us on a road trip from Connecticut to Portland, Maine, and by overnight ferry to Covey Island Boats, in Lunenburg. Nestled along the serene shores of Mahone Bay, the picturesque town in Nova Scotia, stands as a colorful and vibrant canvas painted in bright hues of reds, yellows, and blues, reflecting the rich maritime heritage and its European charm. Rhythmic sounds of boat builders and fishermen at work echo through the streets. From the bustling waterfront to the charming cobblestone lanes, Lunenburg exudes a timeless allure that captivates all who visit the Canadian coast of Nova Scotia.

True to their reputation of being the world's best shipbuilders, these master craftsmen, steeped in the age-old tradition of bentwood lamination, were responsible for constructing the iconic 350-foot Schooner Bluenose 2, a Canadian legend sailing vessel etched on the Canadian dime. The wealth of expertise accumulated over generations of the age-old traditions of shipbuilding along the east coast of Canada was nothing short of remarkable.

The shipyards housed massive warehouses to store multi-ton vessels, schooners, cruising boats, and sailing vessel masts, half a football field in length, beautifully laminated, and polished to perfection. Julia and I experienced craftsmanship of exceptional quality such as we had never seen before. My new friends at Covey Island Boat Works embraced the concept of my invention and, over several months, they worked diligently from the plans, the engineering sketches, and sample limbs. The finished product, beautifully shaped and polished, was shipped in parts to me in Connecticut, not only meeting but exceeding expectations, and effectively demonstrating the validity of the proof of concept and paving the way for initial sales.

With official product in hand, I was able to demonstrate this beautiful tree-like device; described as an upright All-in-One Exercise station, designed of five innovative interactive 'limbs' and handles, with potential to revolutionize the way people move their bodies, using upright convenient exercise for the whole body. With traction generated by WillowWORX for its targeted conditioning benefits, in expos, conventions, investor summits, startup competitions and initial sales across New York, Boston, and Connecticut, the popularity of the device necessitated the exploration of larger-scale and more cost-effective production.

This led me to identify a Chinese manufacturer specializing in Fiber Reinforced Plastic (FRP), offering the ability to replicate the bentwood lamination method at a fraction of the cost. This idea received valuable support from SCORE, an entrepreneurial resource led by retired executives and business strategists who generously volunteer their expertise to assist startups. For all startups and innovators, I recommend a starting point with your local SCORE chapter as they can be very helpful.

My dedicated SCORE consultants, Miki, and Joe played pivotal roles in this journey and eventually became my travel companions as we embarked on an adventure to Beijing, China. Thanks to my connections at SCORE, these two individuals, with whom I collaborated bi-monthly for an entire year, invited me to join them on a trip to Beijing to explore Chinese manufacturing opportunities. Our destination was an established factory owned by Mr. Li, a Connecticut resident with a Taiyuen based factory that specializes in FRP. He also had a USA home workshop which proved valuable to us as we engineered and researched extensively the best method to produce our other newly patented products.

Our journey across continents and cultures, spanning six days in Beijing and Taiyuan, was a delightful blend of humor and exceptional productivity. Under the watchful care of Mr. Li's family, including his wife, daughter, son, and factory executives, we enjoyed the comfort of a six-star hotel and seamless transportation to engineering meetings, cultural experiences, and amazing meals around the clock. Despite language barriers, we managed to communicate effectively through a combination of part English, part Chinese, hand signals, sketches, and Google translation. Together, we successfully achieved our goal, with Taiyuan's precision and scalability turning our vision into a tangible product ready for shipment.

The subsequent steps involved self-learning about logistics, international shipping, customs laws, and export codes to facilitate the product's journey from China to the USA. Again, with the assistance of SCORE, and local legal support, we navigated through this process, including obtaining authorized identity numbers, NCAIS, and International Classification codes for the product's purpose, market, function, and material. We even obtained a CAGE code for readiness with government contracts, such as with the military or health institutes. I learned a lot in arranging transportation from China to the New York shipping port of entry and coordinated the delivery from New York to Connecticut.

The arrival by lift truck that deposited a massive wooden crate, 6 by 6 by 5 feet onto the driveway, marked a suspenseful moment. With crowbars and determination, we cracked open the solid, reinforced ocean freight crate, revealing its contents: limbs and bases made of oak and mahogany faux FRP, matching a wood grain quality. As we unpacked the parts, carefully laying them out on the lawn, the anticipation of success grew, and I felt immense pride seeing my ideas materialize with exquisite precision and quality. This product, crafted with meticulous attention to detail, was ready for assembly and sale.

The relentless pursuit of innovation continued beyond the successful introduction of WillowWORX, with initial sales and the establishment of the company's brand. This ongoing effort resulted in the creation and prototyping of three additional groundbreaking exercise and conditioning products: AnkleSTONE® for feet and ankles, BedROK®, a whole-body platform and BaseROK® an interactive mat. These products and their potential within their appropriate $billion markets of wellness devices for injury recovery and prevention represented a significant leap forward within their respective industries.

To gain a deeper understanding of the production process, I continued to seek the expertise of Mr. Li; after all, he was a Connecticut-based

Chinese manufacturer with over 35 years of experience in Plastics, and FRP and he was located only 45-minutes south of me. Over the course of three years, our collaboration and friendship enabled us to refine and define production methods. Despite language barriers, we all managed to engage in extensive and technical conversations, often relying on translators, drawings, hand signals, and Google Translate. In a pivotal development, Craig's son, Harry, relocated to Connecticut, enhancing our communication precisely at the time I needed to acquire the skills necessary to take over the workshop's production of prototypes and products, of AnkleSTONE and BedROK, and required more technical training from both father and son.

Equipped with a well-stocked workshop in my spacious CT home and driven by a desire to maintain control over the production process, I dove deep into the world of resin manufacturing and FRP. I immersed myself in the intricacies of molds, mica, resin mixtures, scales, fiberglass, patterns, saws, grinders, sanders, Dremel tools, drills, glue, gloves, problem-solving, and countless hours of work. I loved it, but it was very hard work.

The process truly became a source of joy—workshop work! I discovered that being in your own workshop is truly fulfilling once you master it. I wholeheartedly recommend creating a workshop for yourself—it's incredibly rewarding to craft things with your own hands, especially when equipped with the right tools. While I'm relieved to have moved beyond the workshop phase, I have fond memories of those mornings when I eagerly inspected the results of my research and development efforts. More often than not, my response was an enthusiastic, "Oh Wow, fantastic! This worked!" The sense of achievement, despite occasional setbacks, was deeply motivating.

This journey was not without its challenges, including a harrowing incident in which I nearly lost the tip of my right index finger during a rushed sawing operation. The pressure to complete the product for a scheduled demo in Miami with NBA Strength & Conditioning Coach Hex Fasihi led me to hurry, and I learned a crucial lesson: never rush around power tools. Thanks to the swift action and support of my children, I received prompt medical attention and eventually made a full recovery. Throughout this process, I relied on loud affirmations to motivate myself, pushing past fears and obstacles with sheer determination.

Over 14 months of dedicated crafting of these products, I felt like a Maui surfboard manufacturer, sculpting 'boards' of resins but my products had the complexity of being groundbreaking and entirely novel constructs. Initially, I used the 'conventional' or 'unconventional' materials of chicken wire and clay for the initial figure. Some people choose foam to shape an initial vision. I found the method of chicken wire and clay to be very effective, allowing new design to emerge with precision and alterations. With the training of my father and son, FRP production partners, I advanced to hone the skill of creating silicone molds, employing fiber-reinforced plastic resin and fiberglass technology to shape the products in a practical and effective manner. This method allowed me to bring my ideas to life, making them tangible and suitable for production. I incorporated the education from my mentors, reshaped the technique, adjusted the chemistry and production methods over many months to create the successful results.

Workshop experiences confirm the transformative power of self-belief and determination. I successfully transitioned from the workshop stage to partnering with a USA production facility, positioning the products for entry into the global market. I'm grateful for the invaluable lessons learned during my time in the workshop, which propelled me to the next level.

I also had the privilege of sharing my comprehensive workshop production methods with Jack Crane of CONNStep, who stated the magical words, *"I know who can do this for you,"*, which was music to my ears as he facilitated my connection to a valuable Manufacturing Support network and our manufacturer, Canevari Plastics, right here in CT. It was at this point, with the commitments from impactful team members that the company transitioned from the dedication of "Me" to "Us".

CHAPTER 9

Building a Brand—Unveiling Vast Market Opportunities in Orthopedic Wellness

To reach this point—the realization of your ideas, or the transformation of ideas to prototype into tangible solutions or products, whatever the form, whatever your ambition, there are a few uncertainties and doubts that continually test your resolve. It is precisely in these moments of doubt that the strength comes to turn your aspirations into actions and breathe life into your ambitions.

Defining our ideal goals and ambitions is just the first step. It necessitates the courage to step out of our comfort zones, pushing beyond the boundaries of what we once believed possible. This might involve confidently presenting ourselves during performance reviews, showcasing our true potential, or consistently delivering outstanding results in our professional roles or holding on to a vision for a long time, until you arrive at the finished product or result.

So, how do we make it happen?

Over the many years of independent striving, pushing oneself to advance a vision, an entrepreneur will attract others who share their belief in the commercial merit of the designs, and will provide their guidance, skills and talent to the cause, either for discounted fees or complementary, based on foreseeable future potential gains. My experience and consistent advances led me to develop the branding "potential" to capture the exceptional marketing talent of our CMO, Dick Belmont, of Belmont Studios. Together, over the past few years, we have developed a robust marketing strategy to attract other valuable members of the team. The lone entrepreneur became a team of two and then four, and now *many* on our dream team. The transition from being "lone founder" to having a team that I could refer to as "we" with confidence, provided immeasurable relief in having a dedicated team, along for the ride. As we are backed by field tests, quality production, research, and evidence, we, as a team, aim to capture the attention of key stakeholders in the sports and medical health industries. We are dedicated to collaborating with pro-and collegiate sports athletes and trainers, medical professionals, rehab therapists, pain and movement specialists, and sales channel distributors, such the likes of Nike, Anta, Li-Ning, or Adidas, to ensure widespread access to our game-changing products. As we expand our reach and solidify our position in the market, we remain committed to excellence and innovation. Our mission is to make a meaningful impact on the lives of individuals suffering from musculoskeletal issues, both foot and ankle and whole body, or those just wanting to maintain functional and pain free abilities for life and provide them with the tools and support they need to achieve their optimal performance and well-being.

Projecting the key growth markets, exercise devices, wellness apparatus, sports and home fitness equipment are all within our market reach.

Each division has a global CAGR growth rate of at least 4%, ranging from $1.3 billion to $7.8 billion. The USA CAGR is also a healthy 4%, worth $700 million to $3.2 billion, at the time of this writing.

Incredible Market Potential

We all know that for thriving sports revenue, an athlete's well-being is key.

The global and USA fitness equipment analysis shows it is poised for substantial growth, reaching $15.24 billion by 2028. Continuing market size and a 4% CAGR growth rate reveal a Total Addressable Market (TAM) of $7 billion and a Serviceable Addressable market (SAM) of $700 million. This is proving to be a very impressive market.

To break out the $7 billion market further, we focus on the Sports Market size and growth, and discover the global sports medicine devices market will be worth $10.5 billion by 2024 with a CAGR (growth rate) of 8.1%, whereas the foot and ankle device market will reach $5.3 billion by 2025 with a CAGR of 6.4%.

Our company's sports market size includes, within the USA: Pain Management Clinicians 105,200, Athletic Trainers 43,500, Orthopedists 25,000, Podiatrists 15,500, Hospital Rehab 7,300, Outpatient Rehab 12,800, Gyms. Exercise/Training Facilities 50,200, Specialty Retail 81,000, Sports Consumers 145 million, Pro semi-pro and all scholastic sports 1.8 million.

Again, our markets are appealing.

It's not merely about having an idea; it's about taking the first steps, speaking with confidence, and having the courage to define your ideal goals and ambitions, beyond the restrictive boundaries of society. It means promoting ourselves successfully during life's reviews and ensuring that our career and personal environment recognizes and values our unique contributions. It's about striving to be the best version of ourselves, both personally and professionally.

The path to progress is rarely straightforward; it often meanders, presenting challenges that can be exhausting and deflating. It may even be painful at times, but within these struggles lie the rewards—the satisfaction of knowing that we've given our all. Progress may seem slow, like a turtle inching toward the finish line, but with each step, we move closer to our dreams. I have been told many times, it is better to proceed slowly and cautiously, thoroughly in business, to ensure its unpredictable challenges don't knock us down. Within us lies an unwavering force that compels us to rise and continue forward—testing our resilience and determination, which is more of a force than many recognize. This force will attract the right partners for you.

CHAPTER 10

Building a Team—Attracting Partners with 'Skin in the Game'

Building a team isn't just about assembling individuals; it's about finding those special 'skin in the game' partners who are as dedicated and passionate as you are. They are the ones who help transform a vision into a reality, and together, you sculpt your path to success. The ZANEEZ dream team has been growing into an incredible synergy of individuals who share the same vision. The art of attracting partners awaits you at many turns of your own journey.

- **The Genesis of Collaboration**
  Throughout the bustling cities of New York and Boston, and the thriving start-up ecosystems in Connecticut, the energy of Innovation summits and Start Up Accelerators fueled the initial push for promotion to set the stage for what was to come. It was at these many elite investor convention events that the foundations of our business gained validity and began to take shape.

- **The Power of Determination**
  Determination has always been a driving force behind the translation from concept to production. Although unwavering determination

acts as a compass, to align what you do, determination alone is not enough.

- **The Moment of Transformation**

  Pivotal moments must be had to help you evolve. And in between those are sub-pivotal moments in which you bend and steer and adapt and advance. Pursue the relationships and networks that can bring you to advance enough to enjoy a significant pivot toward better strategy or faster results or more successful outcomes, achieved with the simple power of your own thoughts, under your own control. I like to say "visit and pivot" as you constantly adjust the steerage of the business direction.

- **Support from Home Ground**

  As testament to the thriving entrepreneurial ecosystem in Connecticut and Massachusetts, I found invaluable support from day one. My journey was not an entirely solitary one as I eventually gained support from organizations to advance prototype to product. In Connecticut and Massachusetts, organizations: CONNStep and FORGE, M2D2, CT Technology Council, SCORE, Well4Tech, Launch Hartford, RESET Hartford, are available for support and I encourage you to pursue the business foundations and many other organizations who support the continued innovation of your state or location.

- **Expanding Our Dream Team**

  Over time, our team grew and evolved. It is delightful to find yourself in the company of marketing or business strategic wizards. One such moment was when I first met our CMO, Dick Belmont. Mr. Belmont is practically a legend in the marketing world. You may remember him from the Fruit of the Loom campaign, where those grapes and apples come alive to do a spontaneous jig off your underwear label. Fruit of the Loom became a household name, because of him and it is a gift to have him in our corner. He's also represented the likes of Godiva and Stanley, and I think it's safe to say that he knows how to make brands shine; together, we worked tirelessly to define and brand behind the ZANEEZ product line. Knowing that life is not always glamorous, it is fun to remember our first meeting on a day drenched in torrential rain. Introduced by a shared colleague, Dick and his partner, John, and I quickly recognized our synergy and after an intense, informative meeting, we came to the agreement to work together.

At the conclusion of our meeting, we couldn't help but chuckle as I stood up, acting professional and fully committed, to 'warrior on' to the train station, headed into the bustling heart of New York City. However, being from a Ukrainian household, it's practically in my DNA to turn everyday household items into fashion statements, and I had forgotten that I was sporting a colossal, bright orange colored clip, one of those "chip bag" clips, Party sized, at least 6 inches across, pinned to my sweater to close it off from the rainy weather. I remember the silence as Dick and I looked at that giant orange clip, then looked at each other and laughed as we both recognized it to be a true embodiment of my character—able to face any challenge, adapting on the fly, and always on the quest to invent as needed *with* the humor to carry on.

The Power of a Few

In navigating this landscape over years, I find myself surrounded by a unique breed, a handful of individuals who have ventured where many fear to tread. They are the ones who embrace the uncharted territory and thrive. In the unpredictable landscape of entrepreneurship, a select few individuals stand out as true champions. Hitting the jackpot with other strong partnerships, I went on to gain experts and team members in production, national promotion, and operations. Each team member brings a flair to the table. We've got partners for production design and CAD readiness, R&D, Advisors, a Patent Legal Team, and manufacturers who can do wonders with thermoform and injection methods, located in the USA. Building onto that, we gained the work talent of our VP Sales with his network of major league athletes and Olympic champions, a business development director, a fractional CFO and a few digital strategists who know the online world better than most of us know our own kitchens.

Our network grew and we now rub shoulders with entrepreneurial support entities from both the national and international playgrounds as we craft a legacy in the world of fitness and wellness.

Even my four children have been an integral part of this journey, offering unwavering support and becoming valuable assets to the business as spokesmodels, product testers, assistants, and financial advisors. Beyond family, I've been fortunate to connect with those who share my commitment to longevity and success. The art of collaboration is an important practice to your shared vision, and the magic that happens when others engage becomes the driving force behind your team is phenomenal.

CHAPTER 11
Strategies for Success—
9 Key Considerations

1. The Power of Knowledge and Confidence

The interconnectedness of knowledge and confidence, and role as key drivers of achievement is based on the simple fact that they are both cumulative. The more you *know*, the more *confidence* you have.

• *Knowledge as the Foundation*
In the world of business and entrepreneurship, knowledge and confidence are inseparable companions, forming a potent duo crucial for success. Being well-versed in one's field lays the groundwork for creativity and authenticity. The more knowledgeable an individual becomes, the more authentic and recognized their work appears. Knowledge breeds confidence, empowering people to tackle their work with assurance and expertise, ultimately leading to improved performance and a willingness to explore new ideas.

The mantra "fake it 'til you make it" is presented not as a deceptive act but as a strategy to draw upon accumulated knowledge and skills. Remember that uncertainty is a part of the gig, but relying on a solid foundation allows you to navigate.

2. Embracing Challenges with Courage; Crushing Challenges with Consistency

I can recount experiences in the morgue while completing my Doctorate in Clinical Pathology through the Department of Medicine, University of Western Ontario, Canada, shadowing forensic pathologists during autopsies, as I discovered an insatiable thirst for knowledge that would serve well to propel me through these daunting encounters.

I must confess that I likely came by this dissection interest naturally, remembering my childhood episodes of walking down to the beach, along the shores of Lake Huron to find dead fish and a sharp piece of beach glass with which to enjoy 'awesome' dissections of the fish, the highlight being the eyeball and its marble-like cornea that provided a thrilling, yet satisfying 'pop' sound when compressed between two rocks. That was my small exploration before going home for supper. I suppose, not really 'normal' activities but fascinating.

Talk about resilience, the ability to pivot, and the capacity to accept and deal with whatever challenges come one's way. We humans are highly adaptable creatures, able to go to newfound levels of discomfort, and back to comfort as demonstrated when we, anatomy students, having pushed beyond the *first* shocks of the first knife cut in human dissection to quickly being able to discuss upcoming lunch choices, during the dissection. Always being courageous to step into any situation, and keeping it light, for the sake of growth.

These experiences teach that bravery isn't the absence of fear but the willingness to confront it head on. Pushing beyond one's comfort zone leads to a profound understanding of next level resilience of the human spirit. Always encourage yourself to embrace the unknown, challenge your boundaries, and discover the courage that resides within you. The strength of it will always surprise and delight you.

3. Cultivating Confidence; Strategies for Nurturing Confidence

In exploring the nature of confidence, it is wise to highlight that it can be cultivated and nurtured over time, even if it wasn't instilled during early childhood years. Effective strategies exist for building confidence, including positive self-talk, setting achievable goals, celebrating accomplishments, embracing failure as a learning opportunity, seeking supportive relationships, and using visualization techniques, as your skills build.

These strategies empower individuals to reshape their self-perception and belief in their abilities, to keep going with overall well-being. The bottom line is that confidence is a skill that can be intentionally developed throughout life.

4. The Courage to Test Your Ideas

Underscoring the importance of testing one's ideas out in the world, and the necessity of embracing discomfort for the transformative powers of pushing boundaries.

I strongly advocate for the courage to test your ideas, as the world's response can be a valuable indicator of an idea's value. Recognizing the importance of becoming comfortable with *discomfort* will shift your mindset to take calculated risks without fear. Consider discomfort as simply 'unfamiliarity' until it becomes familiar. Go ahead, share your ideas with someone appropriate to give you feedback and feel uncomfortable with the ask. Seen as an opportunity for growth, discomfort is the barometer to confirm you are using powerful and yet unfamiliar catalysts for personal and professional development.

5. Embracing a New Perspective

It can be easy to change our perspective. It only takes a moment. In my mind's eye, I conjure an image within split seconds, whenever I need to power up my perspective and courage. I imagine being on a battlefield, a warrior donning some medieval leather armor, swinging a sword, defending against hostile invaders. The days of such battles were undoubtedly arduous and challenging. However, from my vantage point, seated comfortably in a modern white leather office chair with multiple computers, some digital magic and the internet, the task at hand seems remarkably easier.

By changing my perspective, I transform what may appear daunting into something manageable. Recalling the challenges faced by generations of previous or current lives, such as the challenges of battle, your perspective shifts. When tasks seem overwhelming, I remind myself, like an instant flashback of the resilience of humanity throughout history. The resilience displayed by past generations during wars, pandemics, and other existential threats serves as a powerful reminder of our capacity to adapt and conquer adversity. In comparison, navigating the dynamic business landscape becomes much more attainable.

I often think, "If generations before me have handled battle, and hardship, then I can certainly handle this." This mental shift allows me to approach challenges with a renewed sense of courage and determination, and I simply do it. There is no choice not to; with renewed perspective the task gets accomplished, clearing the path to the next level.

By embracing a positive outlook and drawing inspiration from the triumphs of the human spirit over unimaginable odds, I find the courage to confront challenges head-on. I approach tasks with determination and a belief in my abilities. Embracing this perspective empowers me to overcome obstacles and uncover opportunities.

6. What Type of Kid Are You?

Ask yourself, what type of kid are you? It's often said that our actions as adults reflect the personality traits we exhibited at a young age. Your early experiences play a significant role in shaping your character.

What was your childhood like? How was the family dynamic? Where do you fall in the hierarchy? It is said that 'no sibling has the same childhood, and no child has the same parents', supporting the notion that every relationship and perspective is unique. As the youngest of four daughters, I spent much of my early childhood by my father's side. My mother, understandably busy with my three older siblings, often entrusted my care to him. We became inseparable. I loved going to the Saturday market to buy kielbasa, aged cheddar and blue cheese, smoked meats, and head cheese and then to the barber, or to Sears or for an outing to learn from the many skills he shared with me. This early bonding experience left a lasting impression on me.

In addition, the impact of the number of caregivers played a role in shaping my confidence. Research suggests that the number of caregivers during a child's early years significantly influences their success later in life. In my case, being surrounded by a large and supportive family network enriched my upbringing. The presence of numerous caregivers, including four Grandparents, two parents, fourteen doting aunties and uncles and three older sisters provided love, guidance, and encouragement, fostering my sense of security and self-esteem.

Conversely, the absence of a strong support network, particularly in single-parent households, can limit opportunities and resources for children. It's vital to recognize the impact of caregiver networks and invest in early childhood education and community initiatives to break the cycle of limited support. It is also critical to mentor those around you, to share your positive impact, making support more available to those who pursue or need it.

7. The Role of Hope

Maintaining your personal happiness *set point* is critical to keep you persevering, always, with hope. The human spirit possesses an innate drive to persevere, influenced by factors such as neurobiology and a need for growth. The prefrontal cortex, using neurotransmitters such as dopamine and serotonin, and a growth objective contribute to unwavering determination, that helps you to naturally desire to maintain that personal happiness setpoint.

8. The Synergy of Solitude and Work

Solitude is a powerful ally in the pursuit of your goals. It is in the quiet room, the serene forest, or any space free from distraction that you find your sanctuary—a realm where imagination flows freely, and creativity knows no bounds.

For me, running in the forest serves as an incubator for ideas. The absence of distractions allows my thoughts to take flight and my creativity to flourish. Solitude is more than isolation; it is a sacred space for reconnecting with your inner voice. In an oasis of stillness, self-awareness blooms. Listen to the whispers of your heart and silent mind, as they hold the key to your ideas within.

Solitude alone is not enough. It is the synergy of solitude and work that breathes life into your ideas. Dedication and persistence are essential as you commit to the labor of bringing your creations into existence.

Work and solitude are your allies, providing quiet focus, structure and direction. Your work efforts channel the energy of your imagination into tangible form. Make focus a daily ritual and master your time. Tame the distractions of social media, time consuming chores, or frivolous unsatisfying commitments, instead dedicating yourself to the pursuit of your ideas. With determination, each action propels you forward, defying the limits of what was once deemed possible. Solitude and work become trusted allies, catalysts of transformation that empower you to realize your true potential.

The thrill of accomplishment is amplified amidst solitude and work. You'll experience the thrill of accomplishment—the ecstasy of bringing your visions to life. Every stroke of the pen, brush, or hammer, every conversation held, brochure created, or idea exchanged propels you forward.

With each step, you can defy boundaries and embark on a journey of self-discovery.

9. The Role of Fear: Transcend and Conquer

Fear is a primal response deeply rooted in our evolutionary history. While it once served as a life-saving mechanism, in modern-day tasks fear often becomes an unnecessary barrier. It can paralyze us, disrupt our ability to embrace challenges, and hinder us from reaching our full potential.

Transcending fear means understanding that it is a manifestation of our own energy at a *low vibrational frequency*, aligning with negativity, disconnection, disassociation, discontinuance, and disempowerment. In modern life, these states are often unnecessary. Instead of succumbing to fear, we can choose courage and action. Empowering ourselves with positive thoughts and messages, we can toughen up and face life's challenges head-on.

I experienced the power of conquering fear during my travels in Hawaii and Australia, discovering that even the smallest gesture can embody courage. First, I applied a temporary tattoo that read "NO FEAR" onto my ankle. Sequestering my fear of getting a tattoo, this simple, yet powerful, message resonated with me, propelling me to keep up with the rigors of kiteboarding, white water rafting and bungee jumping, and the "regular" adventures of the week. The point is, words are powerful, and the message really worked.

Empowering ourselves with such simple reminders can be very helpful in overcoming fear and embracing courage. It's a simple and accessible way to tap into our inner strength and choose action over hesitation. As we replace fear with empowerment and confidence, we unlock a reservoir of new positive energy, getting comfortable with being uncomfortable, within reason, putting ourselves "out there" into unknown territory, to advance up and up, one level at a time.

A Recap of Strategies for Success

Achieving your dreams and persevering through adversity requires passion, determination, and strategic approaches. Here's a recap of unique strategies for success:

1. Knowledge and confidence are cumulative
2. Be willing to confront challenges head-on; Discomfort be damned
3. Cultivate positive perception with self-talk. Program your mind to accept only positive 'speak.'
4. Test out your ideas in the world
5. Embrace a new perspective
6. Know who you are and love every part of you.
7. Hope is your superpower, to fuel the human spirit to persevere.
8. Solitude and work are powerful allies
9. Transcend and conquer your fear.

CHAPTER 12

The Power of Resonance— Harnessing Positive Energy

res·o·nance
/ˈrezənəns/

noun
the quality in a sound of being deep, full, and reverberating.

In living bodies, resonance is a phenomenon that occurs when the matching vibrations of another object increase the amplitude of an object's oscillations.

PHYSICS; the synchronous vibration of a neighboring object.

Resonance is a profound concept that holds the key to unlocking limitless potential; it is the awareness of how our energy field interacts with the world around us. Within the context of the human body's energy frequency, denotes the natural vibrational state or frequency at which the body's bioenergetic fields achieve balance and harmony, fostering optimal health and well-being.

A neurobiologist or an individual well-versed in the human body's energy fields understands the intricate systems of electromagnetic and bioenergetic fields that comprise our being. These interconnected fields, often referred to as auras or resonance, have profound links to our physical, mental, and emotional states. By exploring the concept of resonance, one can tap into the inherent potential for healing and vitality. Being conscious of how your body resonates entails recognizing the subtle vibrations and frequencies within you and, with practice, learning to elevate and maintain yourself at a higher energy frequency. This state of harmony can enhance overall health, inner equilibrium, and a deeper connection with the world, unlocking the potential for a more vibrant and fulfilling life.

The Power of Your Resonance

The quote "It's not reality that shapes us but the lens through which we view the world that shapes our reality" is often attributed to Stephen R. Covey, best known for his book "The 7 Habits of Highly Effective People," We are, in essence, beings of energy with immeasurable capacity to shape our reality.

Consider your energy field, when amplified, can extend as far as nine meters in diameter, akin to ripples in a puddle. Positive energy resonates with positivity, enabling us to attract and manifest our deepest desires. The energy is within you and can be affected by you and is felt by others just as you sense their energy.

Understanding that our energy field can amplify is evidence that positive energy empowers us to attract and manifest the desires we hold in our hearts. Indeed, the power lies within us.

Trust in the Unseen

Just as our eyes perceive only a fraction of the electromagnetic spectrum, there are other unseen wavelengths of energy, such as radio, micro, and gamma rays. Likewise, the energy within us is a potent force, capable of shaping the reality we envision. We must trust that it exists, much like we trust in the presence of unseen light waves.

Maintaining the resonance of feelings such as gratitude, satisfaction, happiness, self-love, and self-worth allows us to witness the transformation of our physical reality. Our consciousness and energy serve as magnets, attracting what we need and aligning us with who we truly are. We trust in and benefit from the unseen.

Your physical reality often mirrors your state of being, so endeavor to maintain the resonance of gratitude, satisfaction, happiness, self-love, and self-worth. Your consciousness and energy will attract what you need, aligning you with your authentic self. Trust in this energy, as you would trust in the light you cannot see.

Understanding Our Energetic Nature

Awareness of the frequencies we emit guides us as we live with a mindset of positivity, as our reality transforms into a reflection of our state of being. We possess the power to sculpt our destiny through the energy we radiate into the world. Trust in the strength of your energy.

Think of positivity as a radiant frequency that reverberates, like a harmonious note. Like harmony, positive energy attracts what aligns with it. It is the manifestation of the law of attraction—a magnetic force that draws similar frequencies together, resulting in frequencies that amplifies the energy.

When your thoughts, emotions, and intentions vibrate at a positive frequency, you create a magnetic field that draws solutions, opportunities, and allies toward you. This isn't mere wishful thinking; it's the science of vibrations shaping your reality. This power empowers you to act and achieve your goals.

Our intentions are the blueprints that shape the energy field around us. We can fuse them with the resonance of our desires. The more positive and focused our intentions, the stronger the energy field becomes, attracting experiences that align with those intentions.

Reflect on a challenge you've successfully conquered. Notice how, the moment you shifted your perspective to a positive one, doors began to open. This is the magic of resonance. By aligning your intentions with positive frequencies, you tap into a realm of possibilities that may otherwise remain hidden.

Cultivating Resonance: A Practice of Empowerment

Resonance isn't a mere cosmic phenomenon; it's a skill you can nurture. Fine-tuning your vibrational frequency involves cultivating a mindset of positivity, practicing gratitude, surrounding yourself with uplifting influences, and consciously choosing empowering thoughts.

You are not a passive observer but an active participant. The more you comprehend and harness the awareness of your inner power, the more effortlessly you will navigate challenges, attract synchronicities, and manifest your dreams. Never underestimate the ripple effect of small acts to amplify resonance, because the profound impact of your actions, even the tiniest ripples, can create waves of transformation. Here's proof:

The Story of Sophia Lor'Hen

Long ago, in the vibrant world of my grade one classroom, we, a group of curious six-year-olds and our open-minded teacher, embarked on a scientific experiment to incubate two fertilized chicken eggs. We witnessed the miracle of life as part of our science learning.

As the eggs hatched, revealing two adorable fluffy chicks, the excitement reached a crescendo when our teacher shared the news that if any two students wanted to adopt one of these newborn chicks as a pet, they would need their parents' permission.

My young heart buzzed with the vision of having my own real-life pet chicken.

At home that evening, always eager to bring any animal friend home, I sought the permission required. The first "yes" was easily gained from my mom, who deferred the ultimate decision to my dad. Minutes felt like eternities as we waited for him to return from work. As the clock struck 6 PM, the door opened, as my dad stumbled into the chaos of his beloved household, and with a burst of excitement, I implored, "Say yes, Dad, say yes!"

Initially confused by the request, then feeling overwhelmed after about 35 requests on repeat, my dad finally succumbed to the enchantment and chuckled, agreeing to this heartfelt plea, despite not fully understanding the agreement's content. It was a resounding yes, and my heart soared with joy and excitement, exclaiming, "Yay, we get to have a pet chicken!" My dad, laughed along with us, as for the first time, he realized that we were going to 'have a pet chicken,' an option he had never truly protested, reminiscing about his rich childhood filled with pets and farm animals.

So, the feathered companion, christened Sophia Lor'Hen, became a cherished addition to our family. Sophia's presence brought delight and amusement as she laid her eggs in the most unexpected places, such as the charcoal barbecue or the dog's house, as she became fast friends with the family's cocker spaniel. Laying 336 individual eggs, each carefully counted and marked with a green magic marker by our diligent mother, Sophia was the beloved pet who landed both of us on the front cover of the local paper and proved to me the power of perseverance. The moral is that even at a young age, one can influence the outcome.

Another Remarkable Turn of Events

In another event that would become a defining moment in my adult and entrepreneurial years, my second Cousin Sharon and I embarked on a memorable trip to Boston with an impromptu detour to Gillette Stadium. It was a venture born out of curiosity and a whole lot of that stuff called positive audacity, and it demonstrates the power of determination and seizing opportunities.

Sharon had traveled from Calgary to Connecticut, where I lived, to shop for her wedding dress in Boston. Our plan was to spend the night in Cape Cod and then head into the city for a day of shopping and exploration. As we sat at a restaurant, having cold drinks, hot dinner and chatting with our waiter, we noticed the massive sports complex in the distance. Curious, we asked the waiter about it. He was dumbfounded. "You don't know? That is Gillette Stadium, where the Patriots play football."

We pretended to be knowledgeable, not wanting to confess our ignorance, nor lack of sports interests, both of us attributing it to our recent arrival from Calgary, hiding behind Sharon's cloak of naivety.

We shared a laugh at our little white lie, but armed with newfound knowledge, we headed back to our hotel with a plan in mind.

Turning Curiosity into Action

As we brainstormed and encouraged each other, we decided to seize a grand opportunity the next morning. Our resolution was clear: we were going to Gillette Stadium to introduce the training staff and coaches to the exercise products that I had been developing. It was a bold move, but we were fueled by determination. Afterall, Sharon was a feisty entrepreneur at heart, just like me.

The following morning, we drove all the way back to the colossal Gillette Stadium in Foxborough, Massachusetts. We were on a mission to connect with the decision-makers who could benefit from our products. After assessing the area, we determined that our best approach was through the main store, filled with football-related merchandise, where we would find a sneaky way to the powers that be, whoever they were. Filled with ambition, I led the way at a fast pace, with Sharon skipping behind to catch up. We weaved our way to the back of the store, where we spotted some ominously large rear doors that seemed like an entrance to the offices of the training staff and coaches. As we approached the doors, I extended my hand to push it open, and to our surprise, it swung open as two men emerged.

Seizing the Moment

Instantly questioned about what we were up to, my confidence and determination never faltered as I repositioned my extended hand to shake one of the men's hands and declared our purpose. "Yes, I'm Dr. Zanyk and I have created a very interesting exercise device that your athletes and trainers need to know about", I boldly declared as I handed him a business card and showed him images of our products. To our delight, he agreed that we should connect with the athletic department. and directed us to go straight up to the fourth floor and communicate with the training staff and assistant managers. Grateful for the opportunity, we thanked him and headed around the corner to find the next door of opportunity. After clearing security, we took the elevator up to the fourth floor, where we were greeted by reception. Trembling with disbelief that we had made it this far and were standing in the executive offices of Patriots coaching staff, we requested a discussion about my newly invented product.

While we didn't get a meeting that day, we did manage to leave a written note, thrilled with our accomplishment of making it to the Executive Suites to deliver our information. As we rode the elevator back down, I couldn't resist doing a handstand, much to Sharon's amusement. Something my kids and I would do for silly laughs in an empty elevator. We giggled all the way home at our audacity and the results of our perseverance. Later we had extra bonus laughter in the car as we realized that if any elevator had security cameras, it would be those of Gillette Stadium; we wondered if they would laugh at the bonus handstand.

That day, we both learned that when you push yourself to go beyond your comfort zone, you may face discomfort, but changing your perspective and going for it can make all the difference. It's always worth it to harness positive energy and hold the power of high frequency resonance, with passion and an enthusiastic outlook.

CHAPTER 13

Reading the World—Mastering the Communication of Body and Facial Language

In the pursuit of strategies for success and the enhancement of essential knowledge skills, I highly recommend honing your ability to read body language and micro-expressions. *Thought* is universally expressed through patterns of muscular micro-contractions in facial and body movements. This fascinating area of study is immensely valuable, as it enables you to decipher messages beyond spoken words.

I consider this skill as a "superpower"—an ability to interpret the muscle patterns aligned with neuropsychology, allowing you to stay ahead with the 'unspoken' truth. It is easy to grasp some basic aspects of body language. For example, during business gatherings, when people are *evaluating* your presentation, argument, or project, they typically present one side, usually the right side, of their face. When they *decide in your favor*, there's often a subtle turn of the head to present the other side of the face, indicating agreement and alignment with your message.

The movement that you witness may be as subtle as a tilt of the head, rather than a full head turn, as indication of the thoughts of agreement.

Another fundamental aspect is foot movement. When standing and conversing, it's essential to have a broader view of the whole person, not just their upper body. Observing foot movement can provide insights into the other person's engagement level. For instance, if the person's foot turns slightly, they might be signaling readiness to move on, which means you have about 10 to 15 seconds to conclude your point before they shift their focus elsewhere.

It is informative to become familiar with subtle and not-so-subtle patterns of muscle contractions that reveal emotions like a true smile, contempt, disagreement, or stress indicated by an increased blink rate. To gain a comprehensive understanding, look for clusters of body expressions rather than isolated cues. Experts in neuropsychology emphasize that these subtle yet universal body language actions can hold significant implications in the business world. Nonverbal cues provide valuable insights into individuals' thoughts, emotions, and intentions, facilitating effective navigation of various interactions.

The study of micro-expressions is particularly fascinating. These fleeting facial expressions occur involuntarily and reveal genuine emotions, often before individuals consciously control them. Paying attention to micro-expressions can offer invaluable insights into a person's true feelings and intentions, especially during high-stakes situations or emotionally charged interactions.

Study the anatomy of the face to catch key micro-expressions, present for fractions of a second, and so subtle only to be seen by the practiced including:

Eyebrow Flash: A quick, fast, subtle raise of the eyebrows, signaling surprise or interest.

Eye Squint: A slight narrowing of the eyes, indicating skepticism or suspicion.

Lip Compression: A brief pressing together of the lips, suggesting withheld emotions or hesitation.

Nostril Flaring: A subtle movement indicating irritation or anger.

Tongue Jut: A quick flicker of the tongue against the cheek, signifying discomfort, or contemplation.

Eye Blocking: Covering or rubbing the eyes may indicate discomfort or an attempt to avoid eye contact. When the hand moves, it is often for a reason, not just position shift.

Jaw Clench: A tight jaw, or slight shift of jaw, revealing stress, frustration, or an attempt to control emotions.

Micro Shoulder Movement: Slight shrugging or tensing of the shoulders, conveying uncertainty or doubt, sometimes seen in just one shoulder.

Recognizing these micro-expressions can be challenging since they happen within a fraction of a second. However, by paying close attention during interactions, you can gain a deeper understanding of a person's emotional state, enabling more effective communication and building stronger connections.

The art of reading body language and micro-expressions is a valuable skill for enhancing your ability to interpret thoughts and emotions in various interactions. Using this skill, you can understand the power of nonverbal communication to connect more deeply and empathetically, fostering both personal and organizational growth.

CHAPTER 14

Articulating with Impact—Brevity, Tolerance, and Gender-Based Differences in Language Usage

- *Gender Differences in Number of Words*

  When reading the world, and adapting to diverse business settings, it helps to be aware of natural and evolutionary-based gender differences in daily word usage. On average, men tend to use around 5,000 words per day. In contrast, women can tend to use as many as 25,000 words per day. Of course, some days, depending on mood or situation, we might only say 25 words, but the word counts are a notable pattern, *in general*. This pattern is evident in my family, as it plays out when my daughter and I get together, revealing a high word count, especially when compared to the conversation with my sons, which reveals less words. These numbers provide valuable insights into communication dynamics. Understanding these differences can help you communicate more effectively, especially when addressing gender-diverse audiences.

It's believed that these gender-based disparities in word usage stem from evolutionary roles. Historically, men experienced days of solitary, focused hunting, requiring minimal verbal communication. This naturally led to less word usage among silent individuals. In contrast, women, known as gatherers and nurturers, frequently gathered in their tasks, and exchanged information within their communities. They shared knowledge to benefit themselves, their children, and their family clans. This naturally led to more extensive word usage among multitasking individuals.

- *Embrace Diversity in Communication*
  Approaching the topic of gender differences in word usage takes sensitivity. Individual differences outweigh broad patterns, of course. In our modern world, historical gender roles have evolved, and numerous factors, including personality traits, culture, and socialization, influence communication styles, requiring adaptation to the audience that you are in front of. Effective communication should respect and celebrate the uniqueness of everyone's style. Be aware to tailor yours, as you ebb and flow through life's audiences.

- *The Power of Tailoring Your Delivery*
  Just as the pursuit of excellence in communication involves adapting your delivery when needed, it also transcends with the number of words spoken; By embracing simple communication, to convey complex or brand-new ideas, we can better gain audience understanding and acceptance.

I have found myself in gender-imbalanced audiences many times during Venture Summits and Business Investor events in New York City and Boston. Often, I was one of just three or four women among 40 to 50 men, at the meeting. In Boston, in the Medical Tech industry, I was the only female presenter on stage out of 22 companies, all represented by men. I am aware of the differences in communication style and adjust my communication style accordingly. For example, and this may seem stereotypical, but I have found it to be true—if you're presenting to a group composed mostly of men, it can be helpful to adopt a more concise and direct approach. Think of a solitary hunter with a spear and focus on the sharp point—get to the point quickly. Conversely, when addressing a predominantly female audience, the stereotypical speakers, and gatherers of information, you may incorporate more extensive explanations and anecdotes. I have benefited from my learned ability to streamline my message. A skill always welcomed by any audience and recommended for everyone to practice. Take a three second moment to formulate your answer, before making a sound in answer, as you stay relaxed, and let yourself, at lightning speed, formulate your answer into a better & concise package, with better delivery. *Then* you speak. And you deliver with good cadence, confidence, and poise to land the message to the best of your ability within about three to four talking points.

CHAPTER 15

Gain the Right Perspective— Attract the Audience with Simple Messaging: Sell the 'Job to Be Done', Not the Product

In the world of captivating storytelling, two vital aspects define your success in creating an enchanting narrative. It's all about harnessing the right perspective to draw your audience in. These two aspects are key to unlocking that mystical door and attracting partners, executives, bosses, customers, or consultants to join you on your vision quest.

• The Eloquent Art of Simplification
When standing at the crossroads of complexity and clarity, which path do you choose? Complexity might impress a niche audience, but simplicity embraces the masses. The mastery of transforming intricate ideas into eloquent simplicity is a form of linguistic alchemy that makes even the most bewildering topics accessible. Amazon's Jeff Bezos is an advocate of simple-speak to drive the message.

Why is this significant? Because most people are drawn to ideas they can *effortlessly* comprehend, and to language that bridges gaps and dismantles barriers. When explaining concepts, speak as if you're sharing tales around a bonfire. Unravel complexities into threads of simplicity, connecting hearts and minds alike. This experience took years for me to master, as the messages evolved and developed. Challenging, yes, especially with complex business or science concepts, but necessary.

- Selling the "Job to be Done'
My business story began with the simplicity of nature, yet it took me years to simplify the storytelling behind the brand. For instance, when our CMO and I were tasked with creating the most recent version of brochures, as the User Guide to demonstrate use of our products, first AnkleSTONE and then BedROK, it took us months and months, to streamline the features and benefits, as we were forced to "boil it down", distilling and simplifying our portrayal of the product's essence. It takes a while to be able to answer what it is and what it does for whom and say nothing more. To all who have experienced it, this is a very difficult task, requiring many iterations and focused definitions, to reveal the true bare bones *essence* of the concept.

Imagine having to explain not just the nuts and bolts of an invention, in simple speak, within limited space, but also speak to the dreams it inspires. The option to inspire to, "Stay in the Game," for instance, and not just to offer the 'Only All-in-One Foot & Ankle Conditioning Platform'. Having considered all the claim liability issues to avoid, we have boiled down our answers and state that AnkleSTONE 'supports in the ultimate correct position' with an underlying message of bringing you the *dream for pain free performance in the game of life.*

Regarding AnkleSTONE, our summary brochure of its features and benefits, its methods of use, and why you need it conveys a message that athletes don't just *use* AnkleSTONE to enhance performance, but to *'stay in the game longer'* and *'win more'*. We convey that patients, therapists, and doctors don't just use AnkleSTONE to improve range of motion and alleviate pain, they use it to *'embrace wellness for life.'*

Your offering isn't just a product, it's a solution, a dreamcatcher, a bridge to a better reality. Craft your message not around what it is, but what it enables. Don't just speak; let your words soar on your vision and keep it simple.

CHAPTER 16

Embracing Small Steps— The Significance of Incremental Progress

Achieving success as an entrepreneur isn't an overnight phenomenon. It's a journey of small, persistent steps toward your vision and goals, paving the way to achieving your aspirations. There are no shortcuts or magic formulas; it all comes down to taking one step after another with unwavering dedication.

Each small step may seem inconsequential on its own, but when combined with determination and dedication, they accumulate to create powerful momentum. It's like building a staircase one step at a time, knowing that each step brings you closer to the pinnacle of success. You can't skip the steps. Not one.

It's easy to become overwhelmed by the magnitude of the work, to feel daunted by the tasks and distance between where we stand and where we want to be. However, focusing on the small steps ahead allows progress in which you will find motivation in your achievements, no matter how minor they may seem.

Another great reward from embracing the power of small steps is that we can free ourselves from the paralyzing fear of failure. Instead of being intimidated by the enormity of the tasks that will fulfill our goals, we can concentrate on the immediate actions we need to take, knowing that each small step is an investment in our future success. Moreover, the beauty of small steps lies in their accessibility. We don't need to have it all figured out or possess all the resources upfront. We can start with what we have and gradually expand our efforts as we progress. It's about taking that first step and then the next, trusting that each step will lead to more opportunities and greater possibilities.

CHAPTER 17

Unlocking Success: The Transformative Power of Strategic Mentorship

The incredible impact of seeking mentorship from fellow entrepreneurs is the valuable insight worth sharing that plays a pivotal role in your efforts toward translation into success.

To turn ideas into flourishing ventures, within the intricate landscape of business, there is a need for adept guidance. It's not just about finding any mentor but finding the ones that can help you precisely when you need it.

Connecticut, being a positive place for business startups, offers remarkable resources through organizations such as FORGE, CONNStep, and CTNext, which support the stages of transition of product or business service to reality. To get started, SCORE, the retired business executives who offer support to startups in diverse ways can be key. They were the support I needed to get me to Beijing to establish our first contract for WillowWORX®; I couldn't have done it without them. All of the support groups that I uncovered and benefited from in CT and MA, provide insights that textbooks can't, strategies that are battle-tested, and a network that opens doors you might not even know existed.

Imagine this as a treasure hunt—a search for minds whose experiences resonate with your mission. Whether it's crafting Pro Forma financials, optimizing operations, or architecting a comprehensive business platform, mentors are your treasure map. We cannot know it all and fortunately, mentors will bridge your gaps. Building a business isn't just about products anymore; it's about creating ecosystems, and platforms that offer value beyond expectation. Although my mindset and vision were the driving force, I used mentors to guide me as I molded my vision into a comprehensive strategy. They helped me see beyond our offer of products, adding in training programs and desirable dream solutions that resonate with the end user such as a trainer's goal of a non-injured team, an athlete's dream of winning the gold or a golfer's desire to play without pain; thus, turning new offerings into the cornerstones of a thriving platform.

A well-conceived business strategy isn't a quick sketch. It is composed over a long time. Anything worth having is worth waiting for. Be patient. Strategic mentorship is the culmination of insights gained from mentors who've seen the patterns, lived the challenges, and emerged victorious. Get them on your side.

CHAPTER 18

The Power of Action— Where Seeds Blossom into Results

A profound truth: thoughts that motivate your actions are the architects of your results. Consider your thoughts as the seeds waiting to be planted into fertile soil of action. Actions and logical next steps nourish the seeds. When you take the first steps towards your goal, usually putting your idea into words with someone willing to consider the concept with you, such as my first, casual conversation at a neighbor's barbecue party with a fellow who happened to be a patent lawyer, you *can* gain insight. I received a positive response and this first action, a small step, set into motion a series of events that shaped the rest of the story. Perhaps, for you, it is the first inquiry into a potential customer's challenge, or a strategy idea to improve your efforts at work. Whatever the situation of your ambitions, the first steps will likely set up a series of events that are simply productive, forward gaining tasks.

But it's not just any action that ignites this alchemical process; it's the action fueled by intention, commitment, and purpose. Your sequence of actions isn't a sprint, it's a marathon. It's not a backyard garden but a massive field of vegetables to feed the entire village. The seeds you plant today might not yield fruit tomorrow, but they will eventually, with unwavering patience and nurturing. Your small, consistent actions will accumulate, broaden, and sculpt grand monuments of success. Your daily devotion to your craft, and persistent pursuit of excellence, will shape your masterpiece. Reminding you that every overnight success is ten years in the making.

And during those years, you must unravel the intricacies of success, one action at a time.

CHAPTER 19

Warrior Up for Future Generations—Advocating for Female Leadership

au·dac·i·ty
/ôˈdasədē,

noun

a willingness to take bold risks. *Positive Audacity* involves courage in the face of risk of some kind, such as rejection, embarrassment, or criticism. Purpose-oriented and skillful aspects of positive audacity fully embrace this risk, whereas the more selfish and expedient aspects of negative audacity ignore and may even be blind to risk.

Innovation alone is but a spark; it takes the audacity to fan the flames, to ignite a transformative blaze. Remember, your innovation is nothing without the courage to unleash it upon the world. So, rise above the hesitation and embrace the call to action.

With more audacity, I believe we can create a more equitable world by advocating for female leadership. Picture a world where empowered women stride confidently into significant leadership roles, in equitable representation, shaping an equitable and harmonious future, with incredible talent. To fan the flames of invention and creativity, solutions, and advances, requires positive audacity.

We must "Warrior Up" both for ourselves and for the next generations to come. I believe that our daughters' daughters will hold significant leadership roles in a more equitable world, but we must be the bridge builders across the chasm of discomfort. Embracing the unknown and consistently tapping into the well of incredible powers within each of us. It is in these moments of challenge and uncertainty that your greatness emerges and societal advances break through.

CHAPTER 20

Empowering Dreams— Unleashing Your Inner Dr. Zanyk

Innovation and courage lie only in potential, until you unleash them. Every day, new inventions and creations are concealed within the confines of the human mind. All require pure human power to set them free. This ability surges through our veins but remains dormant unless you whisper it into its vast expanse of possibilities.

It takes more than just brilliant concepts and genius insights to birth innovation; it requires a daring heart to challenge the status quo. The journey from innovation to implementation is a daring dance with uncertainty and always a leap of faith. It demands the strength to confront doubts and the resilience to face failure head-on. Innovation is not forged from the safety of the known; it is a creation born by daring to break free from the shackles of convention.

CHAPTER 21

The Dance of Abundance— Trusting the Flow of Resources

The magical rhythm that beats beneath the surface, in the symphony or *cacophony* of entrepreneurship, beats to the dance of abundance. As an entrepreneur, it's natural to cast worried glances at the financial mountains that stand between you and your milestones. But as someone who dares to dream and manifest itself into reality, let me share some secrets that have woven through my journey and through the journeys of countless others; the universe conspires to support your ambitions.

The Flow of Resources

Money, like water, has a way of flowing to where it's needed. The journey to your business's milestones might seem daunting, with expenses lurking at every corner. But the resources you need will manifest when the timing is right.

It may seem crazy, but it happens.
Instead of fretting about each dollar needed for your milestones, embrace the uncertainty as part of the grand plan and trust in the resonance of abundance. There's a unique magic in knowing that the

universe holds the key to your financial puzzle. As you take inspired actions toward your goals, you'll find that opportunities and resources appear like stepping stones, paving your path to success. Just as the river navigates twists and turns, your own entrepreneurial or business journey will see the ebb and flow of funds that support your progress. I have found this to be an amazing, but true phenomenon.

Using Good Credit: Building Bridges to Dreams

One of the bridges to unlocking financial support is your good credit. Your credit history connects your aspirations with funding. Consider it a tool, not a burden. By using your credit wisely, you're building a bridge that carries you over.

Good credit proves your commitment and reliability. It's not a sign of dependency but a testament to your financial wisdom. While building your dream, there might be moments when utilizing your credit is necessary. It's not a sign of weakness; it's a strategic move that aligns with the greater picture you're painting.

Dancing with Faith in You

As you navigate through the challenges and milestones, remember that faith is your partner in the dance of abundance. Be faithful in your belief of your capacity to embrace the challenges, release the worry, and open your arms to receive the solutions. This dance with faith and belief in yourself isn't about relentless struggle, it's about gaining results from your consistent actions.

Trust that as you work diligently, every step you take, every bit of funds you gather from various corners, every nod in agreement—are the universe's affirmation that you're on the right path. Let go of the need to control every financial aspect, and instead, direct your energy toward your vision.

As you weave your destiny, remember the resources you need are already on their way, and your good credit can be a valuable tool to facilitate your progress. Trust in the dance of abundance, and you'll find that the universe supports you.

CONCLUSION

"Unleashing Innovation"— Embracing Courage and Discomfort

In the concluding chapter, we arrive at a pivotal moment; one, where the threads of inspiration and wisdom converge. It's a call to action, a gentle yet firm nudge towards embracing the forces that drive you to crucial junctures.

Courage: The Catalyst of Innovation

As we reflect on the paths we choose to travel, one-word echoes through the pages of this book, a word that has been the driving force behind every entrepreneurial success story: courage. It's not just a quality we possess; it's the spark that ignites the first step, the spirit to face setbacks, and to persist against all odds. Start with that.

Recall that courage isn't the absence of fear; it's the audacity to act despite fear's presence. It's the conviction that innovation requires daring leaps into the unknown. Ask yourself, if not you, then who? Let courage be your best companion on the road to greatness.

Embracing Discomfort: The Forge of Innovation

Discomfort is the crucible in which innovation is forged as we need that friction to polish our ideas, the pressure that squeezes down upon us, and the uncertainty that haunts us. It's a sign that we're pushing boundaries, venturing beyond the familiar, and challenging the status quo.

We must learn to celebrate discomfort as a partner in our quests. Never fearing it but embracing discomfort as it is in those moments of unease and uncertainty that we grow the most. It's when we step out of our comfort zones that we discover our true potential.

Unleashing Innovation: The World-changing Force

Innovation is not the exclusive domain of tech giants or industry leaders; it resides within each of us. It's the idea that sparks in our minds, the solution to a problem that plagues us, and our novel approach that can transform vast industries or small yet important aspects of your personal life.

Innovation is built by individuals who dare to dream, who are unafraid to fail, and who can go the distance with a vision within reach.

EPILOGUE

"A Journey to Empowerment Continues"—Continue the Pursuit of Your Ambitions

In this epilogue, I'd like to remind you to look at your ambitious goals as an infinite adventure with boundless opportunities for growth and impact. Empowerment isn't a destination but a way of life. It's about continually seeking new horizons, pushing, and embracing the changes that come our way for endless growth and evolution. Carry forward the wisdom of your limitless potential, as your inner warrior is always ready to rise, with innovative spirits eager to create, ... unafraid and strong. In your limitless possibilities, envision a future for yourself that intersects with the collective pursuit of empowerment. It's a future where innovation knows no bounds, as it is not an elusive dream but a reality we craft with our own hands.

"Innovation is Nothing" is a reminder of your own courage, and a blueprint for this future of yours, as you build it—one empowered step at a time.

Now go unleash your inner warrior and live your dream!

www.ingramcontent.com/pod-product-compliance
Lightning Source LLC
Chambersburg PA
CBHW031901200326

41597CB00012B/508

* 9 781968 519414 *